READING COMPREHENSION
PART II

SAT®

ADVANCED
PRACTICE
SERIES

ies
TEST
PREP

Created by
Arianna Astuni, President IES
Khalid Khashoggi, CEO IES

Editorial
Patrick Kennedy, Executive Editor
Rajvi Patel, Editor
Caitlin Hoynes-O'Connor, Editor
Yasmine Gharib, Assistant Editor

Design
Kay Kang, Creative Director

Authors
Arianna Astuni
Emily Blake
Christopher Carbonell
Joseph Carlough
Yasmine Gharib
Chris Holliday
Caitlin Hoynes-O'Connor
Patrick Kennedy
Khalid Khashoggi
Sarah Khashoggi
Paul King
Rajvi Patel

Published by ILEX Publications
24 Wernik Place
Metuchen, NJ 08840
www.ILEXpublications.com
© ILEX Publications, 2014

ON BEHALF OF
Integrated Educational Services, Inc.
355 Main Street
Metuchen, NJ 08840
www.ies2400.com

We would like to thank the ILEX Publications team as well as the teachers and students at IES2400 who have contributed to the creation of this book. We would also like to thank our Chief Marketing Officer, Sonia Choi, for her invaluable input.

The SAT is a registered trademark of the College Board, which was not involved in the production of, and does not endorse, this product.

ISBN: 978-0-9913883-9-4
QUESTIONS OR COMMENTS? Email us at info@ilexpublications.com

TABLE OF CONTENTS

Dear Student:

Right now, educational publishers all across America are gearing up for the Redesigned SAT that will premiere early in 2016. But in the meantime, hundreds of thousands of students are preparing to take the SAT in its present form—and will need outstanding practice material to achieve the scores they desire. We at IES know how quickly students can move through test prep books. And we are determined to give those students who have registered for the 2015, current-format SAT all the resources they require.

That is where this book comes in. For students who completed our original Reading Comprehension workbook, this Volume II is the ideal-follow up. For students who need a crash course in SAT Critical reading, this book offers 22 passages that focus on especially challenging topics in the humanities, history, and fiction. Along with these, you will have the benefit of our popular Online Vocabulary Course and our unparalleled, on-demand Answer Explanations Service. Just contact us at info@ilexpublications.com to make the most of these resources.

We at IES Test Prep have always believed that every student, every score matters: our fifteen-year track record of massive score increases and perfect-2400 scores is the result of this belief. We are all entering a new era in SAT prep, but we are still determined to help those students who aim to take the SAT before the 2016 re-vamp. While this may be one of the last books ever published on the current SAT, it is a necessary book, and a valuable one. Get ready for a new round of practice, and get ready to take control of the SAT —as it is right now.

Sincerely,

Arianna Astuni
President, IES

SAT
Reading Technique

SAT
Reading Essentials

Each SAT Reading Test follows a standard format:

♦ **70 Minutes** to complete **67 Questions**

♦ **Three Sections**, the First **Two at 25 Minutes** and the Final **One at 20 Minutes**

♦ **Five answer choices** per question, **0.25 Point Penalty** for wrong answers

♦ Three Types of Content:

    I.   **Sentence Completion**
    II.   **Short Reading Comprehension**
    III.   **Long Reading Comprehension**

This book is designed as an intensive course in **Long Reading Comprehension**. To explore full, expert-designed SAT Reading Tests, consult the IES *Critical Reading Workbook*.

The Long Reading Comprehension passages on the SAT will adhere to the following guidelines:

WORD COUNT: The long reading passages on the SAT will typically range from 500-850 words, excluding introductory material and footnotes

FORMAT: Each long SAT reading passage will be introduced by an italicized blurb that indicates the passage's content. You will then be given either a single long passage or two paired passages on a single topic. This book deals entirely with single-passage long reading comprehension.

> ✔ **Quick Tip**
>
> Be ready to deal with challenging vocabulary in SAT passages: like Sentence Completion, Long Reading Comprehension tests your knowledge of advanced English words.

CONTENT: SAT passages feature topics in the humanities, sciences, and social sciences; the test also features excerpts from works of fiction and autobiography. This book deals primarily with the humanities and with fiction, which are two areas that many test-takers find especially demanding.

Answering the Questions

*The IES Reading Comprehension Technique is straightforward and effective.
We have outlined the general steps of our technique for you to apply while you
practice these passages. To ensure the best interpretation of these steps, do
not hesitate to consult a teacher or contact us for an online tutorial.*

1. Read the Italicized blurb at the beginning of the passage, NOT the passage itself. Use the blurb to find essential information about the **topic** of the passage and about the author's **intent or argument** in writing the passage.

2. Read the first question carefully. If it has a **line reference**, you may proceed to the next step. If it doesn't, skip it and come back to it once all the line reference questions have been answered. Write down the numbers of all non-line reference questions so that you can return to them easily.

3. For a line reference question, go to the passage and underline or bracket the reference. Read all that you need to read BEFORE and AFTER the line reference in order to fully understand the line reference.

4. Now, you are going to develop your own answer to the Line Reference Question. We will refer to these answers as your **MARGIN ANSWERS:**

   ✔ Quick Tip

   All SAT questions rely on direct evidence from the passage. If you are using your own interpretation of the passage INSTEAD of finding answers that paraphrase its content, you are not answering SAT Reading questions correctly.

   BEFORE looking at multiple choice answers: Answer the question yourself by writing in the margin. Ask yourself these questions:

   ◆ WHO will my answer be about?

   ◆ WHAT action will my answer be about?

   ◆ What will the TONE (+, −) of my answer be?

   You may not use all of these tools every time, but using at least one will help with a quick and precise process of elimination (POE)

5. Go to the answer choices. Never look at the choices before you have formulated a margin answer.

6. Process of Elimination: As you are doing POE, you are not considering every answer choice. Instead, cross out answer choices by locating FALSE WORDS that do not match your Margin Answers. Make sure that you do not jump to the answer choices before your margin answer has been fully formatted.

7. Non-Line Reference Questions: Once you have finished the questions that have line references, return to the questions that do not have line references. By this point, you will have worked extensively with the passage and should have a strong enough command of its content to answer these questions quickly and confidently.

Note to Teachers

Be sure to reinforce the steps in the IES method. Students of different levels may encounter different problems. Watch out for the most common mistakes made by them when using this technique:

♦ Over-generalized Margin Answers

♦ Reading too little

♦ Reading too much

♦ Not reading the question discerningly

♦ Not following the question prompt (ie: imply, infer, suggest, primary purpose, etc…)

♦ Being subjective (not using visual clues)

♦ Ignoring or misinterpreting tone

♦ Using the answer choices to formulate Margin Answers

Need an answer explained? To help you work with our passages, IES offers an online answer explanation service. Simply send the page number and question number that you need explained to **info@ilexpublications.com**, and we will contact you with a breakdown of the question.

Part 1

Questions 1-13 are based on the following passage.

"Free running" is a sport that involves racing on foot and overcoming obstacles in terrain. In this passage, the author explains the role of free running in the life of one contemporary young man.

The first time you meet Paolo, a spry twenty year-old, your impression may deceive you into thinking that he is just another youth emerging from his teenage
Line years and living in a suburb of Rio de Janeiro. Jeans
5 and T-shirt and sneakers, some piercings and tattoos, a three-day stubble, and no trepidation about standing his ground when challenged, he enjoys clubbing with his mates. Sometimes, he stays up all night. He has his iPhone and he likes his music loud. With a cursory *casual*
10 glance, you might well label him the kind of person who makes the members of an older generation feel a little insecure and mutter to themselves that they don't know what today's youth is coming to.
A more perceptive eye would notice other things.
15 There is a sense of controlled strength in the way he holds his body. His movements are purposeful, lithe, and economic; these are movements that denote an athlete. When you chat with him, he responds softly, yet firmly and precisely. His eyes look at you directly.
20 They evaluate and consider intelligently, and when Paolo smiles, he does so with encompassing warmth. You realize that you are talking to someone who has already known both difficult and blissful times and who is determined to use his varied knowledge of life
25 in his future development. Paolo is clearly a young man who is going far—and not solely with the aid of his feet.
Paolo focuses his remarkable stores of energy on free running, an activity often confused with the
30 sport of parkour. This is understandable since, on the surface at least, the two have similarities. Parkour came first: it is a sport that involves finding the fastest and most efficient way of getting from A to B, that is, in a straight line with no deviation on account of
35 the terrain. Sebastien Foucan, the world's foremost exponent of parkour, learned from his father, who created the concept while training soldiers in the French army. Foucan's friend and rival in this sport, David Bell, developed free running, which some
40 people call "fancy parkour." For Bell, parkour's sole focus on speed and direction precluded opportunities for individual runners to express their own feelings and personalities. Each person's body has a certain individuality; thus, since there is often more than one
45 way to overcome an obstacle, free running allows each runner to create a highly personalized art of movement.
Paolo felt this vocation for the first time at twelve years old, when he saw older boys on swings, leaving
50 the seat mid-flight, rolling backwards through the air, and finally landing on their feet on the ground. When

he finally recreated this acrobatic marvel on his own terms, he experienced a real sense of discovery: he felt wonderfully different from everyone else. Those older
55 boys were impressed and, eventually, one of them showed Paolo how to do a back flip off a wall, opening doors to other aspects of free running: precision jumping, using the force of momentum, adjusting direction through the twisting of the airborne body,
60 switching between horizontal and vertical movement, adapting the vaults and flips learned at the gym in order to boost power and speed and to cover more space and scale greater heights. Paolo's initiative had led him into a new world.
65 To the outsider, watching Paolo train is rather like watching a ballet dancer rehearse. Paolo himself would not take the description as far as that, but he does admit that break-dancing can be seen as a similar form of self-expression. He records videos
70 of his "rehearsals" and later adds music to them and puts them online, where they already boast a modest following. Okay, he agrees, some people call it "just showing off." But then he explains that "in a way, you could say the same thing about David Beckham," the
75 famous athlete. "He's got style and he knows it and he shows it. That's why he is who he is." Paolo knows that some people are wary of free running because it is dangerous and involves scaling walls and leaping from roofs, activities that bring to mind daredevils, rebels,
80 even burglars. When questioned further, he shrugs and asks "Why conform to what society wants?"
Paolo knows what he wants: he wants to make a career of free running. He wants to be a stuntman. He knows that his path will not be easy, that his actions
85 can be dangerous, that his luck has been plentiful so far—just a few sprained ankles and bruised bones. He knows that there's a lot of competition, too, and a lot of red tape before he can make it into the profession. He knows he has to give up some things in order to
90 get what he wants: he had a girlfriend when he was thirteen but, in the end, they broke up because he spent more time on free running than on her. He also knows that, if he does succeed—and he will—he will have achieved his dream.

1. The passage as a whole is best described as

    (A) a refutation of the negative stereotypes that
        surround young people in contemporary
        society
    (B) a persuasive discussion of the shortcomings
        of parkour and the virtues of free running
    (C) a description of a young man who has found
        an unexpected outlet for his talents
    (D) a parable about the need to challenge political
        and economic norms
    (E) an impressionistic study of the destructive
        effects of individualism

2. In context, the function of the first paragraph is to

   (A) illustrate the growing generational rift in England
   (B) present an image that is challenged later in the essay
   (C) describe a coherent system of ethical principles
   (D) pinpoint regions where particular stereotypes are prevalent
   (E) encourage readers to disregard commonplace interpretations

3. The author's statement in lines 22-25 ("You realize...development") characterizes Paolo as

   (A) sheltered but fundamentally ambitious
   (B) guided mainly by his instincts
   (C) capable of learning from his past experiences
   (D) motivated by a thirst for adventure
   (E) eager to escape his limiting past

4. In the second paragraph, the author's attitude toward Paolo is

   (A) apprehensive
   (B) appreciative
   (C) ambivalent
   (D) rhapsodic _enthusiastic_
   (E) merciful _forgiving_

5. The author refers to "Sebastien Foucan" (line 35) and "David Bell" (line 39) in order to

   (A) argue that two modern sports are virtually indistinguishable
   (B) praise the enduring friendship between two very different sportsmen
   (C) imply that free running will soon render parkour obsolete
   (D) indicate that personal tensions often motivate innovations in athletics
   (E) provide a brief account of the development of free running

6. In lines 57-63 ("precision jumping...heights") the author lists

   (A) some of the skills and aptitudes that free running requires
   (B) activities that only expert commentators would understand
   (C) interpretive movements that express grace and sensitivity
   (D) the most important free running techniques developed by David Bell
   (E) minor differences between free running and parkour

7. Lines 65-69 ("To the...self-expression") serve to compare

   (A) free running and different forms of dance
   (B) private motives and external appearances
   (C) incompatible aesthetic and athletic standards
   (D) popular and unpopular spectator sports
   (E) traditional and contemporary performing arts

8. The situation described in lines 69-72 ("He records...following") is most directly analogous to which of the following?

   (A) A folk band wins critical acclaim with its first record, but is largely neglected by casual listeners until its second and third albums appear.
   (B) An athlete plays video games and watches action movies in order to relax before an important championship game.
   (C) A stand-up comedian builds up her fan base by distributing a self-published book, which contains a sampling of her best monologues.
   (D) A singer and songwriter work together on a demo tape, but end their collaboration when they cannot secure a production contract.
   (E) A novelist publishes intricate political novels under her actual name, but also writes inspirational short stories under a pseudonym.

9. In context, lines 76-81 ("Paolo knows...wants?") indicate that Paolo is

   (A) destined for a lifetime of disillusionment
   (B) unaware of society's typical expectations
   (C) able to justify apparently criminal actions
   (D) contemptuous of social decorum
   (E) unconcerned about observing social norms

10. Lines 65-81 ("To the...wants?") utilize all of the following rhetorical techniques EXCEPT:

   (A) simile
   (B) personification
   (C) direct quotation
   (D) rhetorical question
   (E) comparative analysis

11. The statement in lines 86-88 ("He knows... profession") functions primarily to

   (A) mock an individual's idealism
   (B) condemn a bureaucratic policy
   (C) excuse a misanthropic lifestyle
   (D) list a few considerable obstacles
   (E) emphasize the impossibility of a task

12. The author's tone in the final sentence of the passage can best be described as

(A) deferential   *respectful*
(B) cautious
(C) defensive
(D) ironic
(E) optimistic

13. According to this passage, Paolo can best be described as

(A) reckless and rebellious
(B) calculating and shrewd
(C) boastful and elitist
(D) steadfast and intrepid
(E) reserved and cynical

Questions 14-25 are based on the following passage.

This passage is adapted from a work of contemporary fiction. In the episode that follows, Ms. Maitland is the headmistress at a respected boarding school.

Ms. Maitland's jaw was set tight. Her fingers tapped the desk irritably. Her mood had not been leavened at all by her arrival at the school. The
Line caretaker had greeted her with the news that the central
5 heating was on the blink and would have to be turned off for the morning, if not for the whole day. These tidings were followed by e-mails from three staff members, who were all suffering from the flu and therefore absent. Ms. Maitland would have to delegate
10 other instructors to cover their classes.

Ms. Maitland gritted her teeth and turned to the mail on her desk. The first letter was from a parent who hoped it would be alright to take her daughter for a week's holiday in Mallorca, since this was the only
15 time of the year when they could get a cheap flight. This parent felt sure that her daughter would be able to compensate for any important material that might be missed. (The girl was in the bottom set for her year, and very near the bottom of that.) "In any case,"
20 the mother had written, "she will take her books with her and I will keep an eye on her to make sure she reads them." Ms. Maitland gave a sardonic laugh and wondered what the mother would be keeping her other eye on.

25 She pushed the button of her intercom.

"Janet?" She heard a gasp and a sound of hurried scuffling and whispering. "Janet, could you come in? And since I can hear that he is with you, please bring Mr. Boyce with you, if you are both able to spare the
30 time."

Ms. Maitland's lips compressed into a thin grim line; she snapped off the intercom, switched on the coffee maker, and began to take some notes. She heard the door open. She completed her notes and then
35 looked up. Janet, her secretary, stood before her, and positioned beside Janet—a deliberate space between them—was Tim Boyce, grinning with the vitality of carefree youth. He was dressed in sneakers, jeans, a T-shirt printed in lurid colors, and a leather jacket.
40 "Mr. Boyce, I realize that some students may categorize the way you dress as 'awesome,' if that is the word they still use," noted Ms. Maitland. "However, neither I nor the parents are quite so infatuated with your attire as to think it appropriate for
45 a teacher."

Tim strained to suppress a giggle as he shot a sideways glance at Janet, who kept her head averted, although her shoulders bobbed merrily.

Ms. Maitland glared and continued. "It seems
50 that Year 10 is without an art teacher this morning. Please supervise the class. I am informed that they are to continue with their fashion designs for the modern

teenager. I have no doubt that you will be able to give some advice on this particular topic. The bell for class
55 is about to ring, so if you could arrive at the Art Studio before they run riot and absolutely demolish it, I would be grateful."

Tim raised his head as if to protest, but Ms. Maitland's expression was adamant. He shrugged his
60 shoulders, then gave her a beaming smile. "Sure thing, Ms. Maitland. I'll jog all the way. Have a nice day!" He turned and strode to the door, but then turned his head towards Janet. "Catch you later, Jan." Then he was gone.

65 Ms. Maitland's eyes flashed, but she checked herself. "He cannot last," she thought. She turned to Janet and thawed a little. "We have a great deal to get through this morning. Sit down, please, and take notes."

70 Janet said nothing. She pulled a chair to the desk and produced her notepad and pen. Ms. Maitland delivered her instructions in a precise, concise manner. Five minutes later, she paused. She noted the dark circles beneath Janet's eyes.

75 "Is that all quite clear, Janet?"

The girl nodded. "I'll type everything up straightaway."

"There's time for a coffee before we start, I think. I made a fresh pot. You are looking a little fatigued."
80 Ms. Maitland gave a casual laugh. "I shouldn't be surprised to discover that you skipped breakfast this morning."

For a moment, Janet looked directly at Ms. Maitland. Then she grinned. "Out on the town last
85 night. Not the best idea, in retrospect. It won't happen again."

Ms. Maitland's look was quizzical. "Do you mean that it won't happen again this week?" she asked "Or ever, or just with Tim?" Janet was about to respond,
90 but Ms. Maitland continued. "Oh yes, I know: you are grown up now and living your own life, but I do worry sometimes about you, you know. It is only natural."

Janet sighed and smiled. "Yes, I know. But, Mum, I am a big girl now and I have to make my
95 own mistakes." She stood up. "I'll get these typed out immediately, Ms. Maitland." At the door, she turned. "And stop worrying, Mum. Tim and I are not dating. Not seriously. He's nice, but he is too much of a schoolboy for me."

100 "Ah, a bit like your father, then?"

"Oh Mother, not a bit!" said Janet as she left the room, laughing.

Back at her desk, Ms. Maitland smiled, glanced at her calendar, and made a mental note to keep the
105 month of June free.

17

7/12

14. In the first paragraph, Ms. Maitland can best be described as

(A) focused and vengeful
(B) conciliatory and composed
(C) tense and aggravated   *annoyed*
(D) irate and capricious   *fickle, unpredictable*
(E) thoughtful and lugubrious

15. The passage indicates which of the following about the student who wants to take "a week's holiday in Mallorca" (line 14)?

(A) The student comes from a family that has little respect for traditional education.
(B) Ms. Maitland's earlier compassion for the student has been met with ingratitude.
(C) Ms. Maitland believes that the student's real talents have gone unrecognized.
(D) The student is silently resentful of authority figures such as Ms. Maitland.
(E) Ms. Maitland holds the student's academic performance and study habits in low regard.

16. It can be inferred from the statement in lines 22-24 ("Ms. Maitland . . . on") that Ms. Maitland views the student's mother with

(A) hatred
(B) credulity
(C) cynicism
(D) envy
(E) trepidation

17. Ms. Maitland's secretary and Tim Boyce most likely establish "a deliberate space between them" (lines 36-37) because

(A) Ms. Maitland dislikes all displays of physical contact
(B) they view one another with moderate disapproval
(C) they are aware that Ms. Maitland is easily distracted
(D) they do not want to appear to be fraternizing
(E) Ms. Maitland's office is large and commodious

18. In lines 40-45, Ms. Maitland characterizes Mr. Boyce's wardrobe as

(A) miscellaneous and puzzling
(B) unprofessional and slipshod
(C) sophisticated yet incongruous   *inappropriate*
(D) opulent yet repulsive
(E) trendy but unsuitable

fancy, luxurious

19. The reference to Janet's shoulders (line 48) primarily serves to

(A) suggest that Janet is stifling her laughter
(B) imply that Janet is exasperated with Tim
(C) indicate Janet's refusal to hide her emotions
(D) show that Janet is deeply conflicted
(E) establish Janet's flippant personality

20. The tone of Ms. Maitland's instructions in lines 49-57 can best be described as

(A) solicitous and instructive
(B) dry and decisive
(C) overbearing and verbose
(D) authoritative and courageous
(E) vague and uninvolved

21. The passage suggests that Ms. Maitland views Tim with

excessive
(A) exorbitant rancor   *hate*
(B) unqualified esteem
(C) appreciable disapproval
(D) unreasonable distrust
(E) sympathetic optimism

22. In line 71, the word "produced" most nearly means

(A) developed
(B) took out
(C) manufactured
(D) offered
(E) fabricated

23. Ms. Maitland's comments in lines 87-92 suggest that she

(A) is still adjusting to her daughter's independence
(B) does not want Janet's relationship with Tim to be terminated
(C) expects her daughter to embrace an unconventional lifestyle
(D) is oblivious to her daughter's recreational habits
(E) is ambivalent about Janet's defiance of social norms

24. In lines 93-96 ("Yes, I . . . Ms. Maitland"), Janet ultimately addresses her mother in a manner that can best be described as

    (A) carefree
    (B) professional
    (C) enervating
    (D) complacent
    (E) haughty

25. Over the course of the passage, Ms. Maitland's mood changes from

    (A) meticulous to unconcerned
    (B) impetuous to cautious
    (C) belligerent to humbled
    (D) morose to accepting
    (E) irascible to amiable

7/12

Questions 26-37 are based on the following passage.

This passage is adapted from a biographical essay on a major English poet.

Geoffrey Chaucer was born in the fourteenth century around 1343, we think: there are no documents pertaining to his earliest years. However, we do know

Line that his nearest relatives were vintners: they imported
5   wine and resided in Cordwainers Street in London. Chaucer began his working life as a page in the Royal Courts. We know that he was sent to France with the English army and was taken prisoner at Reims in 1359, then released a few months later for a ransom
10   of 16 pounds. He must have been worth something to somebody. His career advanced steadily after this; he became an ambassador for King Edward III and later for Richard II on diplomatic missions to Ireland, Flanders, France, and Italy. He married, lived in
15   the City of London, and held various government positions, including Controller of Customs in the Port of London and Clerk of the King's Works. He died in 1400 and was buried in Westminster Abbey, ending his life as a relatively wealthy civil servant.
20   And an ingenious poet.

During his hectic lifetime, Chaucer wrote not only a series of short poems, but also much longer poems that can almost be regarded as stories in verse, including his greatest work, *The Canterbury Tales*.
25   One might wonder where he found the time.

However, the era in which Chaucer wrote his poems was exactly the right era. Why? Because his works were all composed in English, and until the end of the fourteenth century English was almost
30   exclusively a spoken language: if you could write, then you belonged to the privileged Church and Government elites, so that the languages you used for writing were Latin and French. English was spoken by isolated peasants and uneducated artisans, who
35   really did not count where matters of high culture and government interest were concerned.

Despite the views of the Norman nobility, the English tongue was rapidly developing beyond its origins in Anglo-Saxon. Here is the first line of the
40   great Anglo-Saxon poem *Beowulf*, originally handed down through generations in spoken form and eventually recorded as a written work between 900 AD and the Norman invasion of 1066:

"Hwaet we gardena, in geardagum"
45   (translation: Lo, we have heard, in days of old)

Those of us who have not studied Anglo-Saxon should be confused considerably by this, although we might recognize the two words "we" and "in."

Yet here is the first line of Chaucer's *The*
50   *Canterbury Tales*:

"Whan that Aprille with his shoures soote
The droghte of Merche hath perced to the roote"
(translation: When that April with his sweet showers /
The drought of March has pierced to the root)

55   Well, a reader in the twenty-first century might have difficulties, but with the exception of "soote" the words are much more recognizable. There are some extra syllables at the end of some words and some vowel changes that have shifted a bit in the intervening
60   centuries; however, this is what normally happens when a language develops through speech rather than through writing, which is what happened to the English language and what is still happening to it. To take an example very close to home, teenage language
65   today often seems like a foreign language to people of my more seasoned generation. Rap in particular is a complete mystery to most of us over the age of forty.

Speech is a living form of expression, and just as other living things adapt and change according to
70   need and situation, so does speech. Written language demands a controlled form of communication and is therefore subject to set rules and orders. A pattern of construction is laid down, establishing differences between acceptable and unacceptable forms. All this
75   creates barriers in communication and constraints in conversation, because what one really wants to say can be blocked by standards of polite presentation. English is the most developed spoken language in the world because it has constantly simplified its
80   construction—not as the result of any formal decision, but on account of the essential realization that we need to communicate as directly and vividly as possible.

Chaucer was the first English poet to really understand and report the essential strength, directness,
85   and variety of English. He gloried in both the subtlety and the candor of the language, and grasped the freedom it allowed its speakers and its audience. In one section of *The Canterbury Tales*, Chaucer presents us with a view of a lawyer, an expert in argumentation.
90   And then he adds this observation of the man:

"Nowher so bisy a man as he ther was
And yet he semed bisier than he was."

This is among the most precise and observantly ironic renditions of character that the English language has
95   produced.

Chaucer, for me, is where English literature began. Thank goodness he arrived on the scene when he did, and elevated the state of our native language. In 1400, the King opened the English Parliament for the
100   first time in English, not French. I like to think that if Chaucer had not written *The Canterbury Tales*, things would have been very different.

Who knows? We might all still be speaking French.

26. The first paragraph is notable for its use of

(A) humorous exaggeration
(B) statistical analysis
(C) extended analogy
(D) dramatic irony
(E) biographical information

27. The author asserts that Chaucer "must have been worth something to somebody" (lines 10-11) most likely because

(A) his captors successfully negotiated payment for his freedom
(B) he displayed remarkable tact as a diplomat
(C) his family paid the ransom demanded by his kidnappers
(D) his literary prowess was evident in unexpected situations
(E) it took months for his captors to finally release him

28. The tone of line 20 ("And an . . . poet") conveys a sense of

(A) incredulity
(B) significance
(C) speculation
(D) magnanimity
(E) compassion

29. Lines 27-36 ("Because his . . . concerned") imply that Chaucer's decision to write in English was

(A) idolatrous
(B) ill-advised
(C) elitist
(D) reactionary
(E) novel

30. According to the passage, *Beowulf* (line 40) and *The Canterbury Tales* (lines 49-50) differ primarily in

(A) whether a translator would be able to capture the sense of the poem
(B) the number of identifiable literary allusions that they incorporate
(C) their current popularity among professional scholars of literature
(D) the extent to which their respective languages are identifiable to a modern reader
(E) their reliance on uniquely Anglo-Saxon symbols and metaphors

31. In line 60, "normally" most nearly means

(A) acceptably
(B) plainly
(C) unremarkably
(D) typically
(E) lucidly

32. The author refers to rap music (line 66) in order to

(A) substantiate a claim about the evolution of language
(B) deride a modern musical genre in a flippant manner
(C) comment on the enigmatic nature of a particular type of art
(D) highlight the most obscure traits of a form of entertainment
(E) point out an exception to an established rule of aesthetics

33. As described in lines 68-70, speech is most analogous to

(A) a gaseous substance that is extremely volatile at both high and low temperatures
(B) an alloy that only bends when subjected to remarkable amounts of force
(C) a vaccination that is created to gradually eliminate a common disease
(D) a new bureaucratic measure that consolidates existing administrative procedures
(E) an agricultural machine that is altered over time to better suit the needs of those using it

34. In line 82, "directly" most nearly means

(A) crudely
(B) intelligently
(C) clearly
(D) honestly
(E) authoritatively

35. According to the passage, Chaucer "elevated the state of our native language" (line 98) by

(A) capturing the vibrancy of English with carefully-worded poetry
(B) deliberately adapting new words from French and Latin
(C) writing exclusively in a satiric or ironic manner
(D) expressing dismay at the earlier state of English verse
(E) voicing the concerns and desires of the rising middle class

36. The author's attitude toward Chaucer can best be described as

    (A) evident bemusement
    (B) mild dissatisfaction
    (C) respectful nostalgia
    (D) enthusiastic empathy
    (E) overt appreciation

37. Which contrast best describes how the author views written and spoken language?

    (A) As unambiguous when written, as deceptive when spoken
    (B) As uninspired when written, as subversive when spoken
    (C) As prosaic when written, as revelatory when spoken
    (D) As edifying when written, as disorienting when spoken
    (E) As rigid when written, as fluid when spoken

Questions 38-49 are based on the following passage.

In this passage, adapted from an essay written in 2013, the author considers the building of a church in his hometown of Domfront, France.

~ produce

To most people, the phrase "country village in France" instantly conjures up the image of a group of houses in the middle of verdant pasture, or nestled
Line in the protective curve of rolling hills, or perched on
5 the peak of a stony outcrop. There will be, perhaps, a chateau or a ruined castle reminding the visitor of the village's place in history. Nearby will be orchards, copses, woods, or even forests that hug the banks of a slow moving river winding its way towards the coast.
10 The houses will be close together, half-timbered or whitewashed, lining a cobbled square where a somnolent mongrel lounges in the sun. There will be a bakery for warm fresh baguettes, a small, low-roofed café with its parasol tables where the villagers
15 take their morning *café crème* and smoke and chat and read the paper. There will be a war memorial, and a church, the bells of which will chime the day away. It is a classic and unchanged setting for the visitor. There is a sense of permanence.
20   Domfront, where I live in Lower Normandy, has all these features with one omission: the central church. Established in the early Middle Ages, Domfront does not seem to have had much success with religious structures, despite the fact
25 that the town lies on the pilgrimage road from Paris to the Abbey of Saint Michel on the coast. In the beginning, there were three churches here. Within the castle grounds, you can still see the remains of the Priory of Saint Symphorien which gave comfort
30 and wealth to the Norman nobility and was linked to the great Abbey of Lonlay a few kilometers away to the west. The Priory was pulled down along with the castle by Sully as part of an effort to reduce the power of the nobility in France. Below Domfront
35 and just on the edge of the lower part of the town, are the remains of the Benedictine priory of Notre Dame sur l'Eau, a beautiful remnant, reduced now to an empty shell by the building of the road in the seventeenth century. Now and again, small concerts
40 are given there, but for the most part, it stands chill, empty, and ignored.
        Back up in the old town, there is Saint Julien's plaza. This was where the small Chapel of Saint Julien once stood, serving the townspeople of
45 Domfront. This Chapel was pulled down in the eighteenth century and rebuilt fifty yards away on a wider area, for the townspeople yearned for a bigger church. They should not have bothered, since the reconstructed edifice fell into a state of near-collapse
50 by the end of the nineteenth century. Plans were made to restore the building, but little was achieved in the twenty years that followed. The French law

of Separation between Church and State dulled the religious spirit and the First World War pitched the
55 region into turmoil. When repairs were finally begun, a dreadful storm almost razed the building. This state of disrepair - if not despair - finally came to an end with an ambitious plan to re-build the church. The resurrected structure would be distinguished by its
60 neo-Byzantine design, which means that the church was built not in the traditional shape of a Latin cross, but rather in the square shape characteristic of Byzantine churches. This layout enabled the builders to make the maximum use of the limited space
65 available for the church's site. To cut down the cost, the planners also decided to build the church using the new and relatively cheap material of concrete.
        It took nineteen years to complete the building, in part because the planners decided to add a fifty-
70 one meter spire after the central dome was already built. At the time, it seemed to be a good idea. Domfront's Church of Saint Julien consequently became a prominent part of the local scenery, easily seen from miles away. The church was listed as
75 a landmark in the development of ecclesiastical *of church* architecture in 1993. However, in the end, the weight of the spire was punishing to the concrete supports. The church had to be closed for safety reasons just seventy years after it was completed.
80 A thousand years of civic life in Domfront and no place to worship: it seems rather an ironic comment on the penalties of hubris.
        Yet all is not lost. Next Sunday the bells of Saint Julien will peal out once more. It has cost millions of
85 euros, including subsidies from the European Union, but repairs have been made and the concrete arches have been given extra support. For the first time in years, there will be services in the church again. The local pastry shop has created special cakes for the
90 occasion, the low-roofed cafe across the cobbled way has spruced up its tables and chairs – the somnolent *lethargic* mongrel is already lounging around. This time, may *sluggish* the church last forever.

38. The primary purpose of this passage is to
    unfortunate
    (A) detail the inauspicious history behind the construction of an edifice
    (B) discuss the religious zealotry in the history of Domfront
    (C) describe the neo-Byzantine style of church construction
    (D) itemize the virtues of life in the French countryside
    (E) condemn the political history of a small religious village in France

23

39. In the first paragraph, the author implies that "most people" (line 1) are

(A) envious of French rural life
(B) critical of French cultural attitudes
(C) romantic about French country living
(D) disoriented by the French country landscape
(E) passionate about French architecture

40. The "chateau" (line 6) and the "ruined castle" (line 6) serve as examples of

(A) historical landmarks
(B) tourist attractions
(C) thriving businesses
(D) chronological incongruities
(E) prehistoric architecture

41. The author most likely believes that the French village's "sense of permanence" (line 19) comes from its

(A) invariably agreeable climate
(B) lack of involvement in war
(C) sturdy architectural design
(D) resistance to outside influence
(E) political stability in times of strife

42. The statement in lines 24-26 ("despite the . . . coast") primarily serves to

(A) identify an anachronism in the history of the town
(B) draw attention to a meaningful similarity
(C) extend an analogy concerning relations between Church and State
(D) emphasize the unusual nature of a historical situation
(E) recommend a pilgrimage route that is followed today

43. According to information presented in the third paragraph, all of the following are reasons why the church fell into disrepair EXCEPT

(A) loss of religious fervor
(B) legal contentions
(C) post-war effects
(D) natural disasters
(E) inexpensive supplies

44. In context, the word "despair" in line 57 indicates that

(A) France's political turmoil resulted from the church's refusal to compromise
(B) the town's lack of religious enthusiasm was reflected by the poor condition of the church
(C) a country with a high poverty rate translates to one with a high rate of depression
(D) churches built in the Byzantine style evoke a sense of gloominess not associated with those built in the Gothic style
(E) due to its location, Domfront was especially vulnerable to the aftermath of the First World War

45. The statement on architectural styles in lines 56-63 ("This state . . . churches") serves to

(A) qualify a claim
(B) signal a digression *deviation*
(C) clarify a term
(D) make a contrast
(E) mark an incongruity

46. The author includes the sentence in line 71 ("At the . . . idea") in order to

(A) reflect on modern innovations
(B) indicate the short-sightedness of a course of action
(C) allude to a religious book
(D) establish a political context
(E) praise the civic spirit of the people of Domfront

47. In line 79, the author's use of the word "just" emphasizes

(A) the lengthy building process the church spire underwent
(B) the righteousness the church embodied after the Second World War
(C) the relatively short amount of time the church remained open for worship
(D) the costs and benefits of using concrete to build the supports for the church dome
(E) the short, but convoluted, history of the French village of Domfront

48. According to the author, what is the irony in lines 80-82 ("A thousand . . . hubris")?

(A) Domfront's overly ambitious goal of erecting a stately church resulted in centuries of having no working church.

(B) The French people's dissatisfaction with the French government has led to a separation of church and state.

(C) Although the village of Domfront is on a pilgrimage route, it still does not have a single standing church.

(D) Despite Domfront's morally upright atmosphere, corruption plagues its inhabitants.

(E) Many of the people who lost their lives in the collapse of the church were not pious by nature.

49. The tone of the last sentence of the passage is

(A) playful
(B) vehement
(C) cautious
(D) somber
(E) hopeful

Answer Key: PART 1

PASSAGE 1

15/49

34/49

= 69%

1.	C
2.	B
3.	C
4.	B
5.	E
6.	A
7.	A
8.	C
9.	E
10.	B
11.	D
12.	E
13.	D

PASSAGE 3

26.	E
27.	A
28.	B
29.	E
30.	D
31.	D
32.	A
33.	E
34.	C
35.	A
36.	E
37.	E

PASSAGE 2

14.	C
15.	E
16.	C
17.	D
18.	E
19.	A
20.	B
21.	C
22.	B
23.	A
24.	B
25.	E

PASSAGE 4

38.	A
39.	C
40.	A
41.	D
42.	D
43.	E
44.	B
45.	D
46.	B
47.	C
48.	A
49.	E

Need an answer explained? Send the page number and the
question number to **info@ilexpublications.com**, and we
will send you a full analysis and explanation.

Post-Test Analysis

This post-test analysis is essential if you want to see an improvement on your next test. Possible reasons for errors on the four passages in this section are listed here. Place check marks next to the types of errors that pertain to you, or write your own types of errors in the blank spaces.

LONG READING PASSAGE 1:   # Correct: _10_   # Wrong: _3_   # Unanswered: _____

  ◇ Did not understand the questions or answers
  ◇ Did not understand the line references
  ◇ Read too much or too little around the line references
  ◇ Did not create effective margin answers
  ◇ Did not use process of elimination
  ◇ Could not find evidence to answer the questions
  ◇ Could not choose between two possible answers
  ◇ Could not comprehend the topic of the passage
  ◇ Interpreted the passage rather than using evidence
  Other: _____

LONG READING PASSAGE 2:   # Correct: _7_   # Wrong: _5_   # Unanswered: _____

  ◇ Did not understand the questions or answers
  ◇ Did not understand the line references
  ◇ Read too much or too little around the line references
  ◇ Did not create effective margin answers
  ◇ Did not use process of elimination
  ◇ Could not find evidence to answer the questions
  ◇ Could not choose between two possible answers
  ◇ Could not comprehend the topic of the passage
  ◇ Interpreted the passage rather than using evidence
  ◇ Other: _____

> **Use this form** to better analyze your performance. If you don't understand why you made errors, there is no way that you can correct them!

LONG READING PASSAGE 3:   # Correct: _7_   # Wrong: _5_   # Unanswered: _____

  ◇ Did not understand the questions or answers
  ◇ Did not understand the line references
  ◇ Read too much or too little around the line references
  ◇ Did not create effective margin answers
  ◇ Did not use process of elimination
  ◇ Could not find evidence to answer the questions
  ◇ Could not choose between two possible answers
  ◇ Could not comprehend the topic of the passage
  ◇ Interpreted the passage rather than using evidence
  Other: _____

LONG READING PASSAGE 4:   # Correct: _10_   # Wrong: _2_   # Unanswered: _____

  ◇ Did not understand the questions or answers
  ◇ Did not understand the line references
  ◇ Read too much or too little around the line references
  ◇ Did not create effective margin answers
  ◇ Did not use process of elimination
  ◇ Could not find evidence to answer the questions
  ◇ Could not choose between two possible answers
  ◇ Could not comprehend the topic of the passage
  ◇ Interpreted the passage rather than using evidence
  Other: _____

Part 2

Questions 1-12 are based on the following passage.

This passage discusses American dramatist Arthur Miller (1915-2005) and the historical context of his plays.

The fundamental ideal of American democracy is enshrined in the Declaration of Independence: "All men are created equal, endowed by their creator
Line with certain unalienable rights... Life, Liberty and
5 the Pursuit of happiness." A century later, a brass plate pinned to the base of the Statue of Liberty proclaimed "Give me your tired, your poor, / Your huddled masses, yearning to breathe free." These two quotations entwine to form the basis of what came to
10 be known as the American Dream. Yet ironically, the life of many of the new arrivals in this Promised Land turned out to be very similar to the life they had left behind in other countries. Pursuing happiness was one thing, but capturing it and keeping it was something
15 else altogether.

American dramatist Arthur Miller, particularly in the plays he wrote between 1947 and 1955, attempted to analyze this apparent dilemma. In *All My Sons* (1947) it seems that Miller's protagonist, Joe Keller,
20 has achieved many of the possibilities suggested by the American Dream: a house and a yard with a freshly felled apple tree, family life and relative wealth. As the play unfolds, Joe comes to the realization that, in the apparent fulfilment of his dream, he has in truth
25 compromised his integrity as an individual man. Miller appears to suggest that the irony of "unalienable rights" lies in the fact that, although these rights are tantalizingly desirable to the individual, they are impossible to achieve without loss of the sense of
30 self. Keller's own wife puts the case thus: "Certain things have to be – certain things cannot be. Otherwise anything could happen." Is this really what the Founding Fathers intended? At the end of the play, Joe leaves the stage and shoots himself. Nothing is left but
35 the empty yard and the demolished apple tree, symbols of the tragic effect of the American Dream on the individual.

In *Death of a Salesman* (1949), Miller's analysis goes even farther. Here, Miller considers the
40 bewilderment of the individual faced with the ideal of the American dream by depicting the character of Willy Loman, a travelling salesman. In a series of flashbacks, Willy examines his life-long failure to discover the route that leads to happiness. He
45 thought he had pursued all the correct goals, yet all that remains for him is the fear of abandonment: in particular, there is a sense of alienation between Willy and his son, Biff, who ignores all the demands of conformity that Willy's version of the American
50 Dream entails. The suggestion, perhaps, is that the American Dream is irrelevant to the individual's life, that ambition can compromise the most important of family bonds.

Resistance to conformity is explored further by
55 Miller in *The Crucible* (1955), a play that describes the late seventeenth-century witch hunts in New England, but that uses this context to convey the dramatist's own reactions to modern paranoia. The main character of *The Crucible*, John Proctor, finds himself in direct
60 conflict with the demands for conformity that his community decrees. "A person is either for this court or he must be against it," pronounces Judge Danforth, one of the authority figures in this play. The demands of the state create a system that restricts the possibility
65 of individual dissent and freedom of expression. Proctor sees this clearly: the only way to overcome the demands of the state is to assert the dignity of the individual self. "Because it is my name!" he cries when he refuses to sign a confession of witchcraft.
70 "Because I cannot have another in my life… I have given you my soul; leave me my name."

Miller's plays force us to consider the true intent of the Declaration of Independence. The sense that we have of the American Dream may not have been what
75 the Founding Fathers envisioned when they forged the United States of America. These men were, after all, radically different individuals, each with his own agenda, each with his own view of life. However, they did have one thing in common: they wanted to create
80 a society free from the demands, restrictions, and overbearing class privileges imposed by the ancien regime in Europe. The wanted to forge a country where any person, no matter of what origin, could find the opportunity to advance according to individual
85 ability, education, or talent. It was not naïve to try to create, at the very least, a level playing field. No one can deny the worthiness of that ideal.

Nonetheless, no one can say that the Founding Fathers were universally successful: the Native
90 Americans were put at a long-lasting disadvantage, and it took too long a time before the color of one's skin was no longer a barrier to achievement. The first two "unalienable rights" are "life" and "liberty." Each individual needs to understand the imperative of those
95 two words, for it is easy to forget how fundamental these rights are to the evolution of each of us as an individual. It is only from the presence of these two factors that the third right, the right to the pursuit of happiness, can be attained. We need to be reminded
100 of this if the American Dream is to remain intact, and playwrights like Arthur Miller remind us of exactly that.

1. In the first paragraph, the author mentions the Declaration of Independence and the "brass plate pinned to the base of the Statue of Liberty" (lines 5-6) in order to

(A) imply that America's founding principles were imported from other traditions
(B) encapsulate the fundamental flaws of a system of beliefs
(C) show that moral standards in America have changed radically over time
(D) explain a concept discussed at length in the passage
(E) pinpoint the source of America's exceptional spirit of national unity

2. Which of the following statements, if true, would most directly support the statement in lines 10-13 ("Yet ironically . . . countries")?

(A) In the nineteenth century, Russian immigrants in New York faced working conditions that were virtually identical to those they had experienced in Russian cities.
(B) Before 1920, relatively few individuals of Indonesian descent immigrated to the United States.
(C) European factory workers have historically earned more per hour, but less per year, than factory workers in North America.
(D) Irish immigrants living in the United States between 1850 and 1900 sent much of their income to relatives in Ireland.
(E) For much of American history, average wages have been highest in large industrial cities with access to major bodies of water.

3. In lines 21-22, the author lists Joe Keller's attainments ("a house . . . wealth") in order to

Achievement

(A) educate readers about Arthur Miller's own middle-class lifestyle
(B) imply that Keller's success in life is due to his industrious temperament *diligent*
(C) indicate that Keller's lifestyle appears to be a fulfillment of the American Dream
(D) underscore the superficiality and fragility of Keller's accomplishments
(E) reveal aspects of Keller's life that would have dismayed the Founding Fathers

4. As described in the second paragraph, the "empty yard and the demolished apple tree" (line 35) are best understood as

(A) elements of *All My Sons* that allude to much older plays
(B) artistic choices that the author of the passage regards as heavy-handed and juvenile
(C) motifs that reappear in plays that Miller later composed
(D) symbols that call attention to the dissolute lifestyles of affluent Americans *dissipated profligate*
(E) items of scenery that evoke the dire outcome of a character's choices *terrible*

5. The primary purpose of the third paragraph (lines 38-53) is to

(A) challenge the reader's preconceptions by departing from the main ideas of the passage
(B) set forth an unprecedented interpretation of a canonical American play
(C) suggest plausible and specific real-life models for two of Miller's characters
(D) assert that Miller alienated audiences by insistently revisiting the same themes
(E) offer a further example of Miller's response to the American Dream

6. In the third paragraph, the author suggests which of the following about "Willy and his son, Biff" (line 48)?

(A) Willy and Biff are members of different political parties.
(B) Willy and Biff adhere to systems of values that are deeply incompatible.
(C) Willy's beliefs remain completely ambiguous to Biff.
(D) Willy does not trust Biff to raise a family of his own.
(E) Both Willy and Biff work as traveling salesmen.

7. On the basis of the fourth paragraph, "John Proctor" (line 59) can best be described as

(A) a nonconformist *person not obey*
(B) a polemicist *attack*
(C) a libertine
(D) an anarchist
(E) a hedonist

8. As used in line 77, the word "radically" most nearly means

(A) subversively *disruptive*
(B) vociferously *vehement*
(C) disturbingly
(D) experimentally
(E) remarkably

9. It can be inferred from lines 78-82 ("However, they . . . Europe") that the Founding Fathers

(A) regarded respect for diversity as an idea unique to European politics
(B) wanted to create a central government that allowed for extreme personal liberties
(C) wanted to break with traditions that they deemed undesirable
(D) embraced radical ideologies that shaped their standards of effective governance
(E) disagreed about the best means of overthrowing figures of unjust authority

10. The author most likely remarks that the Founding Fathers were not "universally successful" (line 89) because

(A) Miller's plays egregiously misinterpret "the true intent of the Declaration of Independence" (lines 72-73)
(B) many American historical documents "assert the dignity of the individual self" (lines 67-68) to the detriment of national interests
(C) certain groups were not given a "level playing field" (line 86) by the creation of the United States
(D) Americans today are suspicious of the government and intimidated by the "demands of the state" (line 67)
(E) few American citizens can provide a satisfactory definition of the "right to the pursuit of happiness" (lines 98-99)

11. In the final two paragraphs, the author's attitude is one of

(A) appreciation of the intentions behind the American Dream, but awareness that the Dream has been problematic in practice
(B) conviction that the American Dream has many beneficial results, and exasperation with Miller's highly pessimistic worldview
(C) mastery of the fundamentals of American history, and condescension to those readers who have not attained such knowledge
(D) respect for Miller's accomplishments as an artist, but irritation with the social and political content of Miller's plays
(E) reverence for the Founding Fathers, and personal involvement in problems faced by disadvantaged groups of Americans

12. As a whole, the passage can best be described as

(A) a discussion of Arthur Miller's plays that takes issue with the interpretations offered by earlier literary scholars
(B) an examination of national ideals that makes extended reference to the work of a single playwright
(C) an expression of unequivocal praise for America's past accomplishments and future direction
(D) a rigorous study of the real-life models for some of Arthur Miller's most famous characters
(E) an impartial analysis of the conditions that immigrants to America have faced

Questions 13-24 are based on the following passage.

The following passage is from an essay written in 2013 by a British man living in France. Here the author discusses what it is to be an "ex-pat," a person who has permanently relocated to a different country.

Whether one lives abroad by choice or by necessity, the life of an expatriate is quite a pleasant existence: living and working in a country beyond
Line where one was born and raised provides a very
5 different view of one's original society. You see your country through the eyes of others, feel a sense of freedom, believe yourself to be unfettered from the social mores of your own place of citizenship. As a lifelong "ex-pat," I see only one problem with this
10 lifestyle: no matter where in the world I find myself, all the other ex-pats seem to have gathered together and created "exclusive" clubs, which aid them in clinging rather desperately to all the things associated with their home country. This anxious retrospection
15 prevents any personal growth one could experience as a stranger in a strange land.

Expatriate British like me are the worst offenders in this respect, I am sad to confess. From the Nile Delta to the Cape of Good Hope, from India to the
20 Bahamas, wherever more than a dozen Anglo-Saxons find themselves, they immediately create the Club, replete with its tennis courts, its bowling greens, its library of tattered paperbacks and last week's editions of *The Daily Telegraph*, and the leather-
25 armchaired bar with Gordon's Gin and Schweppes Tonic. Here you will find the ubiquitous "bar bores," with their reminiscences of the good old days "before Independence." On the wooden benches overlooking the cricket pitch, they sit half-watching the match
30 and, in between each command for another round of drinks, explain exactly how the government "back home" has got things wrong "as usual." They always note how the government of the country where they continue to reside is A) incompetent and B)
35 corrupt. They also encourage the visitor from the home country, their voices resounding through all corners of the Club, to beware of the locals, who are untrustworthy and (supposedly) incapable of understanding any instructions given in English.
40 In the entrance hall, beneath a fading picture of the reigning monarch and a drooping British flag, is positioned the respectful native attendant at the desk where one registers oneself and one's chosen "guest"—never a local, of course!
45 "Surely you exaggerate?" I can hear you murmuring. "All that is gone in these modern days." Hardly! I live in Lower Normandy in France, in a small town that is only a hop, a skip, and a jump from the English Channel. Quite a few "Brits"
50 maintain a "second home" here, which they visit

for about three weeks in the year; quite a few other British ex-pats, like me, maintain permanent residency. Even the more permanent ex-pats are instantly recognizable (even though they refrain from
55 hanging British flags from their windows), for they speak to the stallholders in the market in atrocious amalgamated Franglais. There may be no cricket pitch, and the closest thing this town has to a bowling green is the designated *pétanque** area near the local
60 school; however, there is still a Club. It does not fly the Union Jack, nor is there a picture of the Queen anywhere to be seen; rather, it is a local bar with tables and chairs spilling out onto the pavement in that specifically French manner. Sometimes a couple
65 of tables may be occupied by one or two French couples, rather neat and prim, struggling to speak to each other through the noise and ribaldry emanating from the English guests who have commandeered all the other spots. In the main, this is the domain of the
70 expatriate English, where they can sit and comment disparagingly on the French way of doing things, seemingly oblivious but more likely impervious to the fact that many of the French in this town can understand English. Indeed, the French here
75 often speak English more properly than the English speak French. The ex-pats criticize, and loudly, the supposedly quaint customs of the country where they have decided to live, every so often imperiously calling for the waiter to bring another round of
80 drinks, spelling out their orders very loudly and very slowly as if the poor waiter were somehow unable to understand such basic words as "coffee" and "beer." Whenever I stroll around the town, I slink past the Club, hoping that none of the English sitting
85 there will regard me as an errant Brit who needs to be forced to feel at home with his fellow countrymen. From the bottom of my heart, I agree with Groucho Marx: "I refuse to join any club that would have me as a member."

*a sport played with weighted balls on a sandy court

13. The primary purpose of this passage is to

(A) describe the differences between British and French expatriates
(B) lament the uncaring speech and attitudes of other expatriates from Britain
(C) criticize the treatment of expatriates by locals around the world
(D) enlighten expatriates about the benefits of dividing their time between home and lands abroad
(E) disparage British expatriates who fail to support the government at home

14. The phrase "From the…Bahamas" (lines 18-20) serves to emphasize

(A) the varied cultures imported into British society
(B) the most popular vacation spots for British citizens
(C) the trade connections forged by British expatriates
(D) the British tendency to belittle foreign customs
(E) the geographical spread of English expatriates

15. In the context of the passage, lines 22-26 ("replete with…Tonic") present examples of

(A) cultural icons necessary for the continued popularity of British governmental programs abroad
(B) familiar aspects of everyday British life that expatriates use to remain comfortable in foreign lands
(C) discontinued mainstays of British advertising that now can only be found in former British colonies
(D) commonplace items that the author deems necessary when he travels to a foreign country
(E) sports and products that were once only to be found in Britain and that other countries now respect

16. The author's use of quotes around "bar bores" (line 26) and "before Independence" (lines 27-28) communicates a general sense of

(A) disdain
(B) respect
(C) belligerence   aggressive behavior
(D) conviviality   friendliness
(E) melancholy

17. The description in lines 28-39 ("On the… English") suggests that the expatriates who frequent the Club are

(A) compassionate toward the persecuted ethnic minorities in their current home country
(B) perceptive of subtle inconsistencies in their home government's foreign policies
(C) abusive toward the waiters and shopkeepers they know at home in Britain
(D) critical of the culture and government of the country where they reside
(E) apologetic towards their guests concerning the illicit attitudes of the locals

18. The author uses the phrases "fading picture" (line 40) and "drooping British flag" (line 41) to emphasize the idea that the Club is

(A) prominent
(B) dignified
(C) dispirited
(D) secretive
(E) untrustworthy

19. It can be inferred from the second paragraph that the author would most likely

(A) bring local friends to the Club to flaunt his national pride
(B) return to Britain frequently to experience the comforts of home
(C) focus on his work instead of spending time at the Club
(D) avoid socializing with the other expatriates at the Club
(E) steer clear of locals when traveling outside of the Club

20. The "local bar" (line 62) differs from the clubs described in the second paragraph primarily because it

(A) remains a French establishment despite an encompassing British presence
(B) blends various cultures to welcome foreigners of all nationalities
(C) represents a true victory of cultural assimilation
(D) accommodates more locals than it does expatriates
(E) operates solely for the use of British expatriates

21. In context, lines 64-69 ("Sometimes a…spots") present which of the following?

(A) A public altercation   noisy argument
(B) An evident juxtaposition
(C) A groundless caricature
(D) An ambivalent observation
(E) A tentative explanation

22. In lines 69-74 ("In the...English") the author indicates that the expatriates at the Club are

    (A) known to engage the local citizens in cheerful conversation
    (B) oppressively segregated from their surroundings by a parochial local populace
    (C) desperately opposed to the tight moral restrictions of French society
    (D) chauvinistically unwilling to fully integrate into the society in which they live
    (E) routinely mocked in public for their poor French language skills

23. In context, the word "basic" (line 82) most nearly means

    (A) childish
    (B) primitive
    (C) obtuse
    (D) simple
    (E) uninteresting

24. It is indicated in the last paragraph that the author

    (A) still visits home regularly with the other English expatriates
    (B) used to frequent the Club, but has gradually stopped attending
    (C) feels no real desire to be affiliated with the Club
    (D) believes that the other expatriates have fully assimilated to rural France
    (E) is nervous that the other expatriates cannot understand why he left Britain

7/12

Questions 25-36 are based on the following passage.

This passage is excerpted from a historical survey of British drama. Here, the author considers the rise and reception of "Comedy of Manners" plays.

Thirty years after the death of Shakespeare, the performance of plays was forbidden by order of British head of state Oliver Cromwell. This ban was not lifted
Line until the return of the Stuart monarchy in 1660, when a
5 new, very different brand of theatre was instituted. The recently-returned king, the "Merry Monarch" Charles II, had enjoyed years of exile in the more frivolous *silly, foolish* France and was ready to give encouragement to all the delights of the new theatres. Where the king went,
10 society went. It is therefore not surprising that very many of the new plays presented were comedies, and comedies moreover that derived their humour from mocking the manners and foibles of their fashionable audiences.
15 "Comedy of Manners" is the classification that literary critics use for these plays. Wycherley and Congreve were the major seventeenth-century innovators, but this mode of writing has continued through to the present day; critics claim that the
20 popular *Carry On* films are examples of this persistent yet frequently tedious form of comedy. The two main concerns of the genre seem to be the accumulation of wealth and the indulgence of sexual innuendo. While no one would deny that the pursuit of libido
25 and money occupies a great deal of energy and time, such pursuits cannot really be said to give any insight into our existence. Comedy is not just about making us laugh: it is another way of making us consider the human condition. To put it baldly, a pompous man
30 slipping on a banana skin may make the observer laugh, but it is the man himself who feels the pain.
Luckily, there is at least one Comedy of Manners writer who allows us to see how laughter can lead us beyond the artificiality of witty dialogue, who
35 enables us to glimpse the true depths of the human condition. That man was Richard Brinsley Sheridan and his life was, to say the least, eventful. Sheridan was born in Ireland in 1751, moved to England with his theatrically-inclined parents, eloped with a young
40 heiress, bought a share in the Royal Theatre with her money, and eventually became the owner of the same theatre. He also became a Member of Parliament, where he often made brilliant, witty speeches. He even defended the American colonists when they
45 were proving troublesome to the British Government, clearly indicating that he was on the side of the Angels rather than that of the Angles.
Sheridan wrote several comedies, all of them successful in their time. He loved the wit and depth of
50 language, not only what words reveal in their day-to-day usage but also what they can reveal of character or psychology in their rhythm and sound. Here is the first

line of his greatest play, *A School for Scandal*, spoken by a character named Lady Sneerwell:

55 "The paragraphs you say, Mr. Snake, were all inserted?"

evil: hostility

Hear how the ironic use of alliteration brings out the suggestion of malevolence and venom below a seemingly polite enquiry. Compare this with the
60 opening lines of *The Importance of Being Earnest*, a highly-regarded comedy of manners written by Oscar Wilde in the late nineteenth century:

"Did you hear what I was playing, Lane?"
"I didn't think it polite to listen, sir."

65 There is no real complexity beneath the surface of the wit, just a small joke to relax the audience. Wilde's play is regarded as one of the high points in the history of the Comedy of Manners, but it is only a series of set pieces that allow the characters to pronounce witty
70 aphorisms, often without any revelation of inner life or movement of plot. The names that Wilde gave to his characters are all taken, quite haphazardly, from the names of towns on the southern coast of England. Sheridan gave his characters names that reveal their
75 stark personalities: Mr. Snake, Mrs. Candour, Sir Benjamin Backbite, Lady Teazle. Beneath these superficialities lie the characters' real identities, for Sheridan explores the ways we perceive ourselves and others within our native societies.
80 The genius of Sheridan in his Comedies of Manners is to push his audience beyond the mere recognition of the foibles and attitudes paraded by the world of appearances, to foster true understanding. He makes us realize the fragile uncertainty which is within
85 all of us, and which compels us to perform when in the presence of others. At heart, we know that each of us is alone, struggling to discover who we are and how we fit into this strange world. We cover our fears, and transform our lives into moving exhibitions of
90 bravado.
Sheridan did so himself. When his theatre in Drury Lane caught fire and burned to the ground, Sheridan was ruined financially. On the night of the fire, a friend found him in a coffee house across the
95 road, glass of wine in hand, regarding the disaster. Sheridan looked up and said, gently:

"A man may surely be allowed to take a glass of wine by his own fireside."

Now, *that* is Comedy of Manners.

25. The dominance of comedy in seventeenth-century England was most likely "not surprising" (lines 10-11) because

   (A) the nation's popular entertainment reflected the jovial temperament of the king
   (B) the strict policies of Oliver Cromwell had been despised by most inhabitants of England
   (C) Shakespeare's lively sense of social comedy guided later generations of playwrights
   (D) few seventeenth-century audiences were interested in serious or tragic subjects
   (E) France had influenced England culturally before the return of Charles II

26. The tone of the statement in lines 27-29 ("Comedy is…condition") can be best described as

   (A) earnest   *serious, grave, sincere*
   (B) facetious   *playful*
   (C) pugnacious   *aggressive*
   (D) admonishing   *warning*
   (E) celebratory

27. The last sentence of the second paragraph ("To put…pain") primarily serves to

   (A) imply that physical comedy was used extensively by Comedy of Manners playwrights
   (B) highlight the spirit of callousness that is evident in much slapstick humor
   (C) illustrate how a simple comic incident can be accompanied by a more sensitive analysis
   (D) establish a motif that appears repeatedly in Comedy of Manners plays
   (E) differentiate between the experience of the audience and that of the performer

28. The author provides a brief biography of Sheridan in lines 37-47 primarily in order to

   (A) encourage the reader to emulate Sheridan's industrious and ambitious personality
   (B) succinctly describe Sheridan's unique style of drama
   (C) cast doubt on claims that Sheridan's previous biographers have made
   (D) convey the scope and quality of Sheridan's achievements
   (E) spark interest in Sheridan's unconventional political views

29. The author quotes two plays (lines 52-64) in order to draw a contrast between

   (A) characters who embody vice and characters who adhere to simple values
   (B) the lax morality of Sheridan's culture and the more rigorous virtues of Wilde's
   (C) a nuanced and suggestive use of sound and an accessible moment of comic relief
   (D) the calm opening of Sheridan's play and the scene of subtle tension that begins Wilde's
   (E) the childishness of *A School for Scandal* and the evident sophistication of *The Importance of Being Earnest*

30. What do lines 66-73 ("Wilde's play…England") suggest about *The Importance of Being Earnest*?

   (A) It lacks depth and nuance, despite its popularity.
   (B) It rejects the innovations of the Sheridan masterpiece *A School for Scandal*.
   (C) It is set in large part on the southern coast of England.
   (D) It is less popular today than it was at the time of its first performance.   *engaging, absorbing*
   (E) It is more engrossing and entertaining than the plays of Wycherley and Congreve.

31. In line 75, "stark" most nearly means   *sharp*

   (A) disconcerting
   (B) unadorned
   (C) eminent
   (D) bleak
   (E) striking

32. According to lines 83-90 ("He makes…bravado") Sheridan's plays are noteworthy because they

   (A) help their audiences to appreciate realities that are often confusing and alienating
   (B) are designed to leave their audiences with feelings of philosophical despair
   (C) encourage viewers to shed their fears and acknowledge their differences
   (D) were inspired by insights and dilemmas that were unique to Sheridan
   (E) condemn members of the audience for failing to be honest about their foibles

33. "True understanding" (line 83) most directly refers to

   (A) "insight into our existence" (lines 26-27)
   (B) "the artificiality of witty dialogue" (line 34)
   (C) "indulgence of sexual innuendo" (line 23)
   (D) "the surface of the wit" (lines 65-66)
   (E) "exhibitions of bravado" (lines 89-90)

34. The author includes the quotation in lines 97-98 primarily in order to

   (A) praise the calm demeanor that Sheridan normally exhibited in distressing circumstances
   (B) offer insight into the fragility of Sheridan's career and finances
   (C) allude to a type of joke regularly employed by Comedy of Manners playwrights
   (D) exemplify a style of comedic expression that the passage construes as superior
   (E) imply that Sheridan differed from other dramatists in his ability to confront everyday situations with humor

35. It can be inferred that the author believes which of the following about the Comedy of Manners?

   (A) It is ultimately incapable of providing an escape from harsh realities.
   (B) It is most valuable when it exposes human frailty.
   (C) Its focus on salacious topics was new to seventeenth-century audiences.
   (D) It was created to reflect the unusual artistic and dramatic tastes of Charles II.
   (E) Its mockery of social elites initially alienated many theatre-goers.

36. The plays of Richard Brinsley Sheridan are most similar to which of the following?

   (A) Improvisational sketches that rely on elaborately-constructed props to suggest realistic settings
   (B) Animated films that use simple character names to help very small children improve memory skills
   (C) Interpretive dances that use exaggerated gestures but still reflect struggle and uncertainty
   (D) Educational skits that are structured as short conversations about everyday tasks and dilemmas
   (E) Stand-up comedy routines that emphasize provocative social and political themes to entertain audiences

Questions 37-49 are based on the following passage.

The following passage is an excerpt from a short story set in the Germany.

The taxi pulled away, and the silence of the early, Bavarian, November morning surged back. Klaus glanced across the road. The land descended quite
Line sharply to a terrace flanked by council houses, each
5 one silent and gray. No lights were lit. No whiff of smoke ascended from the chimneys. These dwellings could have been abandoned, he thought, they were so impassive. Beyond them, he could just make out the deserted fields that lay along the banks of the small
10 river, itself hidden by a sullen mist.

He thought of the noises and the colors of early morning in the Ethiopian town he had left so urgently, just twenty-four hours before. At this time of the day, the road in front of his house in Africa
15 surged with women in brightly-patterned scarves, with babies strapped to their backs, balancing on their heads straw baskets filled with vivid fruits. Scrawny children in torn shorts and vests ran ahead, behind, dodging through the chattering women—kicking up
20 the red earth in clouds of laughter.

Klaus turned to face the cottage. He pushed the little wooden gate hard. It opened stiffly, grating across the narrow concrete path. The last time he had been here, he had promised that he would replace
25 the supporting hinges, but—what with one thing and another—he had forgotten to carry out his promise. He would do it tomorrow when he got back from the hospital. He put the small case down on the front doorstep and fumbled in his pocket for the key to the
30 door.

Inside, on the floor of the porch, was a small pile of letters that had been pushed through the letter box. Automatically, Klaus picked the letters up. The envelopes all had little windows through
35 which the addresses could be seen. Nothing but bills and demands. He sighed and placed everything on the little shelf beside the door, on a pile of similar, unopened communications that lay there. He pushed open the inner door to the living room, only to be
40 faced with an exhibition of exhausted debris.

The room was cold and silent. In the fireplace were the remains of a deadened fire, ashes spilling onto the grubby tiled hearth. The old television set stood in the corner, its back blocking much of the
45 light that filtered through the latticed windows. Facing it, on the sagging sofa, lay a crumpled dressing-gown, an abandoned novel, a few squashed cushions, and the faded carpet. A stained coffee table supported a mug half-filled with cold and congealed
50 coffee, a battered pair of spectacles, and a small folder from which several photos spilled across the table. Dust was everywhere. He glanced at the clock on the wall: it had stopped.

There was a tap on the front door. He turned.
55 It was the young woman who lived next door. She looked at Klaus, timidly.

"I heard the taxi." She spoke quietly. "I thought you might like a cup of tea."

"Thank you. I just got in. It has been quite a
60 journey."

"Yes. It must have been difficult." She paused. "She didn't want to leave, you know. It was only when the Health Office told her they had gotten hold of you and you were on your way that she agreed to
65 go. She could be very stubborn."

"Yes, she could. Always. All my life."

"Yes. I can imagine." The young woman smiled, in reminiscence. "But she was very proud of you. She always told us about what you were doing, out in
70 Africa."

"I didn't write enough."

"She told us how busy you were." The young woman paused. "Were you in time?"

He looked at her, puzzled. "In time? I came
75 straight here and I'm not planning to see her until this afternoon."

The young woman grew pale. Then the color rushed back into her face.

"Oh! I didn't realize. You haven't been there,
80 yet." She steeled herself. "They rang early this morning. I am so sorry. She—she passed away. I thought you had come here from the hospital. I thought you knew."

He heard her. For a moment that seemed to
85 stretch much longer, he could not comprehend what she had said, but only stared at her. She was trying to keep herself poised, a little awkward but expectant. He tried to find the words that she seemed to need to hear. None came.
90 The silence lengthened. Then she turned away, embarrassed. "I'll leave you. If you need anything, please, just ask." He heard her close the front door.

He crossed to the table and picked up a photograph, looked at it for a moment, and then let it
95 fall back among the others. Then he straightened his shoulders and walked out the front door, leaving the house his mother had abandoned.

37. The first paragraph is primarily intended to

    (A) describe everyday realities, then switch to one of the main character's extravagant fantasies
    (B) provide essential information regarding the setting, then establish a dour mood for the narrative _gloomy_
    (C) introduce the setting in an unbiased manner, then shift to satiric depiction of a specific lifestyle
    (D) focus on the protagonist's point of view, then emphasize the perspective of an entire community
    (E) present a strong thesis about a particular place, then suggest Klaus's ambivalence about this milieu

38. Lines 11-20 ("He thought…laughter") are especially notable for their

    (A) ominous atmosphere
    (B) use of specific memories
    (C) sense of social concern
    (D) analysis of cultural tendencies
    (E) moments of lighthearted humor

39. The first two paragraphs of the passage suggest a contrast between

    (A) the idealism of Klaus's worldview and the dreariness of his surroundings
    (B) the solemnity of Germany and the liveliness of Ethiopia
    (C) the clarity of Klaus's observations and the confusion of his emotions
    (D) the clutter of a European town and the sprawl of the African countryside
    (E) the appeal of communal activity and the necessity of self-reliance

40. Lines 21-28 ("Klaus turned…hospital") indicate that for Klaus, replacing the hinges is

    (A) a rather low priority
    (B) a source of anxiety
    (C) a frustrating task
    (D) a veiled obsession
    (E) a needless diversion

41. The description of the room in lines 41-53 establishes a mood of

    (A) ostentation
    (B) pessimism
    (C) irritation
    (D) desolation _bleakness_
    (E) contempt

42. In context, "deadened" (line 42) most nearly means

    (A) repudiated
    (B) extirpated _destroyed_
    (C) quenched
    (D) weakened
    (E) confounded

43. The young woman's attitude in lines 54-58 ("There was…tea") can best be described as

    (A) philanthropic
    (B) euphoric
    (C) fulsome
    (D) distraught
    (E) solicitous

44. In lines 68-70 ("But she…Africa") the young woman indicates that

    (A) Klaus's family takes great pride in its cosmopolitanism
    (B) Klaus's reasons for not writing were greeted with compassion
    (C) the community often waited eagerly for new messages from Klaus
    (D) Klaus's mother was respected despite her stubborn character
    (E) Klaus's achievements were held in high regard by his mother

45. Line 71 ("I didn't…enough") conveys Klaus's

    (A) awareness of his detachment from his mother
    (B) desire not to be regarded as introverted
    (C) inability to form strong emotional bonds
    (D) dissatisfaction with his present itinerary
    (E) wariness when meeting new acquaintances

46. It can be inferred from lines 79-83 ("Oh! I…knew") that the young woman

    (A) expected Klaus to avoid his mother's house for as long as possible
    (B) was embarrassed by her initial reaction to Klaus's presence
    (C) doubted that Klaus could handle the news of his mother on his own
    (D) assumed that Klaus knew of his mother's death on his own
    (E) was determined to show Klaus kindness despite his evident animosity

strong hostility

47. The description in lines 84-89 ("He heard…
came") primarily suggests that

(A) the interactions between Klaus and the
young woman have become uncomfortable
(B) Klaus has found his conversation with the
young woman to be irksome _annoying_
(C) Klaus normally makes an effort to express
himself in a succinct fashion
(D) the conversation between Klaus and the
young woman could become adversarial
(E) Klaus needs to attend to obligations that
preclude further discussion

48. The passage as a whole is best described as

(A) a redemptive depiction of a deeply
conflicted protagonist
(B) a cautionary tale focusing on the theme of
filial neglect
(C) an explanation of a professional decision
with dire consequences
(D) a conciliatory dialogue between two
estranged individuals
(E) a narrative that features responses to a
personal loss

49. Which of the following statements is most
strongly supported by the final paragraph of the
passage?

(A) Klaus is desperate to leave Germany at the
next available opportunity.
(B) Klaus's actions are motivated by resentment
for his upbringing. _childhood_
(C) Klaus does not wish to spend additional time
revisiting his mother's house.
(D) Klaus does not feel that his trip was a
valuable or edifying experience.
(E) Klaus's affection for Africa may soon extend
to his hometown in Germany.

Answer Key: PART 2

Part 2

36/49 = 73%

PASSAGE 1

1. D
2. A
3. C
4. E
5. E
6. B
7. A
8. E
9. C
10. C
11. A
12 B

PASSAGE 3

25. A
26. A
27. C
28. D
29. C
30. A
31. E
32. A
33. A
34. D
35. B
36. C

PASSAGE 2

13. B
14. E
15. B
16. A
17. D
18. C
19. D
20. A
21. B
22. D
23. D
24. C

PASSAGE 4

37. B
38. B
39. B
40. A
41. D
42. C
43. E
44. E
45. A
46. D
47. A
48. E
49. C

Need an answer explained? Send the page number and the
question number to **info@ilexpublications.com**, and we
will send you a full analysis and explanation.

Post-Test Analysis

This post-test analysis is essential if you want to see an improvement on your next test. Possible reasons for errors on the four passages in this section are listed here. Place check marks next to the types of errors that pertain to you, or write your own types of errors in the blank spaces.

LONG READING PASSAGE 1:   # Correct: _8_   # Wrong: _4_   # Unanswered: _____

◇ Did not understand the questions or answers
◇ Did not understand the line references
◇ Read too much or too little around the line references
◇ Did not create effective margin answers
◇ Did not use process of elimination
◇ Could not find evidence to answer the questions
◇ Could not choose between two possible answers
◇ Could not comprehend the topic of the passage
◇ Interpreted the passage rather than using evidence
Other: _____

LONG READING PASSAGE 2:   # Correct: _11_   # Wrong: _1_   # Unanswered: _____

◇ Did not understand the questions or answers
◇ Did not understand the line references
◇ Read too much or too little around the line references
◇ Did not create effective margin answers
◇ Did not use process of elimination
◇ Could not find evidence to answer the questions
◇ Could not choose between two possible answers
◇ Could not comprehend the topic of the passage
◇ Interpreted the passage rather than using evidence
◇ Other: _____

> **Use this form** to better analyze your performance. If you don't understand why you made errors, there is no way that you can correct them!

LONG READING PASSAGE 3:   # Correct: _7_   # Wrong: _5_   # Unanswered: _____

◇ Did not understand the questions or answers
◇ Did not understand the line references
◇ Read too much or too little around the line references
◇ Did not create effective margin answers
◇ Did not use process of elimination
◇ Could not find evidence to answer the questions
◇ Could not choose between two possible answers
◇ Could not comprehend the topic of the passage
◇ Interpreted the passage rather than using evidence
Other: _____

LONG READING PASSAGE 4:   # Correct: _10_   # Wrong: _3_   # Unanswered: _____

◇ Did not understand the questions or answers
◇ Did not understand the line references
◇ Read too much or too little around the line references
◇ Did not create effective margin answers
◇ Did not use process of elimination
◇ Could not find evidence to answer the questions
◇ Could not choose between two possible answers
◇ Could not comprehend the topic of the passage
◇ Interpreted the passage rather than using evidence
Other: _____

Part 3

3/9

Questions 1-9 are based on the following passage.

The passage that follows is taken from a collection of related short stories. In the episode provided below, Gregory, a man about thirty years old, takes a brief vacation in order to escape his day-to-day worries.

It had not been, Gregory decided, the most intelligent decision he had ever made. While it had seemed like a good idea at the time, he was certainly
Line not laughing now.
5   He had reached the small hotel the previous night. Though weighed down and exhausted when he had arrived, he had arisen the next morning to the fresh, rejuvenating light flooding through the little window. He had leapt out of bed, showered, dressed, and eaten
10 breakfast with a vigor he had not felt in years.
        During his morning walk, he had found the little path beside the creek that trickled down the hill. The hill had not been too difficult to mount, and it was not long before Gregory reached the higher elevation of
15 the moors. In every direction, the purple-tinted heather stretched away, seemingly limitless, until it touched the soaring sky of the horizon. For the first time in months, he felt free and confident. It was as though with each step of the climb he shed one more of the
20 arguments, the worries, the demands, the moments of lonely poverty that his life had accumulated over the years. He gazed around delightedly, then he flung his arms out as far as he could and ran forward, feeling the laughter bubbling up inside him, feeling transformed
25 into a child again, dashing free.
        Eventually, he stopped and leaned against one of the rocks, panting and giggling. He stared up at the clear light. When was the last time he had felt like this? Perhaps it had been that moment when, finally
30 unencumbered by work and family, he had set foot in rural India and embraced the welcoming warmth of that ancient earth for the first time. Everything had seemed possible then, just as it did now.
        All day, he wandered carelessly on the moors, not
35 really bothering about direction. He watched lizards dart across the rocks. He rolled in the heather and lay on his back, regarding the butterflies that skittered around him and the birds that sailed on the currents of air high above. He closed his eyes and listened to the
40 subtle vibrations of the land and the distant barking of dogs.
        It was rain that woke him. The sky had darkened and the wind had grown frigid. He pulled his jacket closer to his body and looked around. The moor
45 seemed different now in the dusk, almost treacherous in its vast uniformity. He stood up stiffly and set off in what he thought was the right direction. The rain intensified. His feet and hands were numb. He stopped and peered around. He had no idea where he was.
50 He found shelter under an overhanging rock face and pondered what to do; he could not simply stay here on

the moor and hope to be rescued. Here he was, alone and out of reach, blundering through this dark and empty vastness.
55   He set out. How long he travelled though the darkness, he did not know. To begin with, he felt only the lash of rain and wind against his sodden body; eventually, he just accepted his discomfort and found ways to put his outward afflictions out of mind. He
60 held imaginary conversations with all those people he had deserted in the past, reasoning with them, patiently informing them that what he had done had been justified. Each attempt at explanation petered out: his attempts always had. He felt only his own exhaustion
65 and then, quite unexpectedly, he found himself falling. His head came into contact with something hard and he lost consciousness.
        He awoke to find a hot tongue persistently but gently licking his face. For a moment he submitted,
70 then stirred himself. A blazing light dazzled him and he promptly shut his eyes. He heard a voice.
        "You're not dead, then? I thought you were at first. Nasty fall, that; lots of deadly patches in these parts. You're lucky the dog found you. Come on. It's
75 time to come out of the darkness and join the land of the living again."
        Gregory thought about this for a moment, the land of the living, and then relaxed. Perhaps it was time.

1. Which of the following best describes the relationship between the first two paragraphs?

   (A) The first paragraph explains the immediate sources of Gregory's discontent, while the second paragraph references scenes from Gregory's upbringing.
   (B) The first paragraph alludes to a dilemma that Gregory faces, while the second paragraph returns to a slightly earlier series of events.
   (C) The first paragraph praises Gregory's prudence and intelligence, while the second paragraph criticizes his unduly optimistic world-view.
   (D) The first paragraph presents a philosophical conundrum, while the second paragraph offers a more pragmatic view of life.
   (E) The first paragraph describes a course of action that faces Gregory, while the second paragraph outlines specific steps for successful implementation.

2. In lines 5-10 ("He had…years"), Gregory experiences

   (A) weariness, which is soon replaced by buoyancy and vitality
   (B) disillusionment, which is soon overcome by new ambitions
   (C) invigoration, which is soon defeated by despair
   (D) annoyance, which is soon countered by renewed focus
   (E) confidence, which soon gives way to recklessness

3. Gregory's attitude in lines 18-25 ("It was…free") can best be described as

   (A) gregarious *sociable, friendly*
   (B) blithe *casual, indifferent, unconcerned*
   (C) petulant *bad-tempered*
   (D) nostalgic
   (E) profligate *wasteful*

4. In line 31, "rural India" is best understood as

   (A) a location where Gregory enjoyed material prosperity
   (B) an area that few of Gregory's acquaintances will ever visit
   (C) the site of most of Gregory's formal education
   (D) a region that offered Gregory a new perspective on international cultures
   (E) a place where Gregory had experienced a carefree sense of liberty

5. What aspects of "the moors", as described in lines 34-41, are of particular interest to Gregory?
   open upland = heath
   uncultivated

   (A) The customs observed throughout the region
   (B) The unparalleled biological diversity
   (C) The carefree and easygoing inhabitants
   (D) The indigenous wildlife and serene landscape
   (E) The possibilities of intrigue and adventure

6. In line 59, the word "outward" most nearly means

   (A) unique
   (B) physical
   (C) ostentatious *showy, pretentious*
   (D) flagrant *blatant, obvious*
   (E) peripheral *outer, surrounding*

7. The author suggests that Gregory held "imaginary conversations" (line 60) in order to

   (A) mitigate the feelings of guilt that his memories stir up
   (B) figure out what he will say to explain his conundrum to others
   (C) better understand his new surroundings
   (D) distract himself from an unpleasant turn of events
   (E) justify life choices that most people would not have made

8. It can be inferred that the statements in lines 72-76 ("You're not…again") are spoken by
   dangerous

   (A) an individual familiar with the treacherous terrain of the moors
   (B) a hotel official who has been sent to find Gregory
   (C) an imagined figure from Gregory's past
   (D) another tourist who is fearful of falling into danger
   (E) a professional member of a local reconnaissance team

9. As a whole, the passage can best be described as an account of

   (A) an explanation of one man's embracing of a cosmopolitan lifestyle
   (B) the animal species indigenous to a little-visited region
   (C) an excursion that leads to moments of pointed self-analysis
   (D) the undesirability of travel in a new and unfamiliar culture
   (E) a serious dispute with a surprisingly comic resolution

a short trip

6/8

Questions 10-17 are based on the following passage.

In the following passage, the author discusses the "slavery footprint" of every individual, and how we can work to reduce global slavery.

Consumerism is on the rise: we want more, we want it fast, and we want it cheap. Our landfills are growing as we accumulate and quickly disregard
Line more possessions. So it shouldn't come as a shock to
5 know that our carbon footprint is getting larger. But most people are unaware that our slavery footprint is expanding as well. This happens whenever we buy products that in some way support modern slavery. If you own a computer, a decent number of shoes, or a
10 bike of just about any sort, you probably have somewhere in the neighborhood of 100 slaves working for you.

A recently launched website called slaveryfootprint.org, which is backed by the U.S.
15 State Department, defines a slave as "anyone who is forced to work without pay, being economically exploited, and is unable to walk away." Through this site, we can calculate how connected we are to human trafficking and slave labor. Knowing that we
20 might have a hand in perpetuating such evils, we should at least take a moment to think about the consequences of our role in consumer society.

The site offers a survey that, when completed, determines the exact slavery footprint of any given
25 visitor. Participants in the survey feed in information about their lifestyles and purchasing trends, and a sophisticated algorithm calculates where geographically their possessions were made. After that, the site searches its database to estimate the
30 prevalence of slavery in these areas and produces a number representing the slavery footprint. The results are staggering. The average person has about 27 slaves working for him or her, and half of those slaves are active at any given moment. This means
35 that the majority of the products we use on a daily basis has at some point passed through the hands of a slave.

With roughly 30 million slaves in the world today, chances are that most of what we buy has at
40 one time or another come into contact with a slave. Chocolate, though processed and packaged by fancy European boutiques, is made from cocoa beans which are gathered by the small hands of slave children across West Africa. Leather from India is often
45 obtained by the forced labor of lower-caste workers. The Thai seafood industry relies on the labor of Cambodian, Burmese, and Malaysian slaves. Coltan, a superconductor used in electronics such as cell phones, is mined by slaves in the Democratic
50 Republic of the Congo. Even in the cosmetics industry, tens of thousands of Indian children mine mica, the little sparkles in makeup, and China's

migrant population often produces the silica in nail polish. And these are only a few of the products we
55 come across daily that depend on slave labor.

This does not mean that all the companies we patronize endorse slave labor, or knowingly run sweatshops. Nor does it necessarily mean that we should vilify a company upon finding out that it is
60 somehow connected to slave labor. What we need to do is understand the supply chains at the heart of the problem; most companies rely on other companies for processed and raw materials, unaware sometimes of where those companies get their materials. We as
65 consumers have the obligation to do the research, and it is incumbent on us, as the end-users of these products, to bring modern slavery to the attention of influential companies. Only if we can rally together and do this in a large way can we have a shot at
70 combating slavery.

On the Slavery Footprint website, users can download the "Free World" software and use it to research brands and stores. Users can also send letters to various companies, requesting inquiries
75 into their supply chains. Companies that receive these letters, fearing negative press about their links to slavery, are more likely to check whether or not their suppliers are in fact utilizing slave labor. Nothing mobilizes business more than the threat of
80 a public relations fiasco. But steps toward a solution can't start until consumers become more aware of the problem.

For most people, slavery is something that happens in distant places, or only happened long ago.
85 But slaveryfootprint.org brings this affliction to our doorstep, and reminds us that by staying unaware and inactive, we are complicit in slavery today.

involved in illegal activity

10. The overall purpose of this passage is to

   (A) highlight certain industries that should be boycotted
   (B) blame people for being knowingly involved in illegal actions
   (C) raise awareness of a corporate culture that willingly participates in modern slavery
   (D) demonstrate that a contemporary problem is insidious yet not insurmountable
   (E) deride the greed and consumerism prevalent on the internet

11. The author uses the term "carbon footprint" in line 5 in order to

(A) introduce the author's thesis in the specific jargon of a scientific discipline
(B) create an analogy between two seemingly disparate environmental concerns
(C) use the rhetoric of a well-known problem to introduce a lesser-known one
(D) explain the connection between humanitarian struggles and the U.S. State Department
(E) illustrate the impact of human civilization on the natural landscape

12. According to the passage, a "slavery footprint" is an estimate of the

(A) consumption of products made by unpaid workers under forced labor
(B) use of items assembled by jailed slaves from overseas
(C) number of geographical regions where slavery still exists
(D) percentage of slaves associated with large corporations
(E) size of the average website that tracks incidences of slave labor worldwide

13. Slaves, according to the site slaveryfootprint.org, are defined as those who

(A) work longer hours than they would prefer
(B) secretly volunteer to work without compensation
(C) are required to work without remuneration   *money paid*
(D) are below the minimum legal age for employment
(E) are not legal residents of the countries in which they work

14. In context, the phrase "hand in" in line 20 most nearly means

(A) responsibility for
(B) role in
(C) investment in
(D) knack for
(E) grasp of

15. In the fourth paragraph, the author develops the main argument of the passage by

(A) analyzing the productivity of slave-dependent nations
(B) listing every national economy that depends on slavery
(C) demonstrating the widespread prevalence of slavery
(D) describing anti-slavery programs in various countries
(E) suggesting a course of action that will combat slavery

16. The author's prescriptions in the fifth paragraph center on

(A) technological research
(B) police investigations
(C) journalistic propaganda
(D) letter writing campaigns
(E) grassroots protests

17. In the last paragraph, the author concludes the passage by   *suggest, call attention to*

(A) alluding to modern misconceptions about slavery
(B) contrasting past and present forms of slavery
(C) confronting the reader with a rhetorical question
(D) substantiating earlier claims with a personal anecdote
(E) casting doubt on the popular appeal of a program designed to combat slavery

Questions 18-29 are based on the following passage.

Adapted from an autobiographical account, this passage describes how its author dealt with an unexpected personal change.

When I was a kid, I used to hate going to the barber's for a haircut. It was torture having to balance on a couple of cushions so I was at just the right height
Line for the barber to deploy his clippers. I squirmed and
5 wriggled and jittered until the barber got irritated. "If you don't keep still, I can't cut your hair. If you don't get your haircut regularly, one day, I promise you, it will all fall out!"

I think I put my tongue out at him. Certainly, I got
10 a smack on the back of my leg from my mother for being rude. What did that barber know about hair? All he did was cut it. Later, as an independent teenager, if I did recall such moments of defiance, I would shrug my shoulders, fling back my flowing Mick Jagger locks
15 and remind myself that no one in my family had ever gone bald.

Cut to Christmas, many years later.

I was going home for the holidays. In the spirit of generosity befitting the season, I went to the hair
20 stylist for a trim. It would please my mum, at least. I no longer fidgeted in the chair: in fact, I was almost dozing off when the scissors stopped mid-snip. The stylist straightened himself and looked at me through the mirror.
25 "Do you know, sir, that you have a bald spot, just here?" He pressed his finger against the nape of my neck. I sat up, verging on panic. "You shouldn't worry. It's probably a result of overwork and stress. Quite a few of my clients have this from time to time, but
30 perhaps you should see a doctor, just to be sure."

You bet I saw a doctor.

"Ah yes, Alopecia Nervosa," the doctor informed me smoothly. "Caused by iron deficiency and stress. Quite common really."
35 I tried to control the quaver of shock in my vocal chords. "And I will recover?"

He shrugged, "Any baldness in your family?" I shook my head in energetic denial. "Well, I imagine it will grow back, eventually."
40 I swallowed and then nodded in what I hoped was a nonchalant manner. "Is there anything I should do?"

He shook his head as he wrote out a prescription. "You should take one of these each day. And just relax as much as possible. It will probably get worse before
45 it gets better, though still, I wouldn't worry about it too much."

Not worry? I recalled that scene from my childhood, and felt as though that barber's curse had come terribly true.
50 I spent Christmas watching my hair fall out faster than the Christmas tree shed its needles. Sure, I went to a few parties, but I soon tired of friends glancing

quickly yet inquisitively at my hair, resolutely averting their eyes, and smiling very determinedly at my chest.
55 In the end, I forced my mother to shave my head completely. She was very reluctant to do so, and with good reason. I discovered that, stripped of its hair, my head revealed an appalling affinity to the low dome of Neanderthal man. I tried to avoid mirrors: I had never
60 realized before how many there were in my mother's house.

Not the happiest Christmas season, indeed. I set off back to London, to work. It was quite chilly—as my head constantly reminded me—but at least the
65 crowds were thin, meaning that almost nobody would be around to notice my strange shorn scalp. I entered the nearest Tube station and descended to the platform below. The area was deserted, save for one other passenger, a young boy about eleven or twelve years
70 old. He glanced at me and then did a double-take. I set my shoulders square and walked farther down the platform. I was aware of the boy's constant stare, yet I was set on ignoring him.

"Mister!" I turned my head. The boy was now at
75 my side, staring fixedly at my head. "Mister, are you a Punk?"

I glared at him. His eyes were not hostile, only excited. I relaxed a little. "No, I'm not a Punk."

For a moment, his face fell, but his gaze never left
80 my head. "Well, you look like a Punk." There was a kind of awe in his voice.

I gave a half smile. "No, I'm sorry. I am not a Punk. I have been a bit ill and my hair had to be shaved off. But I am getting better now."
85 He moved back a step and looked away, his face flushed, embarrassed that he might have been rude. Then he hunched his shoulders, faced me head-on, and looked at me earnestly. "You know, I think you'd make a really good Punk."
90 I felt suddenly lighter in spirit. "Oh. Thank you very much!" I grinned confidingly at him. "I also hate going to the barber."

The boy gave a broad grin. "So do I!"

We shook hands solemnly as the train arrived. The
95 curse was broken.

18. The passage can primarily be described as

(A) a dispassionate analysis of a minor crisis
(B) a wry account of a personal turning point
(C) a whimsical reflection on a rite of passage
(D) an anecdote embellished with slapstick comedy
(E) an easygoing parody of a universal experience

19. In line 4, "deploy" most nearly means

(A) facilitate
(B) send
(C) use
(D) arrange
(E) exploit

20. The barber's statement in lines 6-8
("If you...out!") is best characterized as

(A) an admonition
(B) a recrimination *accusation*
(C) an aspersion *vilify. denounce*
(D) an allusion
(E) a suggestion

21. The tone of the question ("What did...hair?") in
lines 11 is

(A) inquisitive
(B) callous *cold, insensitive*
(C) rueful *regretful*
(D) didactic *instructive. informative*
(E) dismissive *unworthy of consideration*

22. The reference to Mick Jagger (line 14) serves to

(A) introduce an extended analogy
(B) emphasize another case of personal
misfortune
(C) foreshadow the narrator's professional life
(D) provide the reader with a point of comparison
(E) criticize the narrator's apparent role model

23. Which contrast best describes the respective
attitudes of the narrator and the stylist in
lines 25-30 ("Do you...sure")?

(A) Rebellious versus resigned
(B) Anxious versus exasperated
(C) Deferential versus domineering
(D) Headstrong versus solicitous
(E) Alarmed versus unperturbed

24. The narrator's reference to his "vocal chords"
(lines 35-36) serves to

(A) establish the severity of the author's ailment
(B) suggest a sense of tension and distress
(C) underscore the author's aversion to
conversation
(D) anticipate a diatribe that the author later
delivers
(E) demonstrate the narrator's unlikely optimism

25. The narrator uses which of the following in
lines 50-51 ("I spent...needles")?

(A) Analogy
(B) Euphemism *polite term*
(C) Understatement
(D) Allusion *suggestion*
(E) Paraphrase *rewriting*

26. The narrator's friends smile "very determinedly"
at his chest (line 54) most likely because

(A) they do not want to reveal their aversion to
his lifestyle
(B) they are embarrassed by his social ineptitude
(C) they feel disdain and contempt for his new
appearance
(D) they have experienced extremely similar
predicaments
(E) they are trying to avoid making him
uncomfortable

27. According to lines 55-61 ("In the...house"), the
narrator most probably views his decision to shave
his head as

(A) childish
(B) imprudent *unwise*
(C) antisocial
(D) facetious *flippant, treating serious with inappro-*
(E) reclusive *isolated* *priate humor*

28. In line 65, "thin" most nearly means

(A) anaemic
(B) gaunt
(C) sparse
(D) lightweight
(E) narrow

29. Over the course of his encounter with the "young
boy" (line 69) the narrator's attitude changes from

(A) condescension to conviviality *disdain* *friendliness*
(B) trepidation to animosity *fear* *hostility*
(C) inquisitiveness to humiliation
(D) defensiveness to solidarity *unity*
(E) obliviousness to affability *friendliness*

Questions 30-41 are based on the following passage.

In this passage, the author discusses the life and significance of Mary, Queen of Scots (1542-1587).

As far as history is concerned, I am a romantic, not a scholar. The dates and treaties and movements that apparently created the world I live in today are
Line extremely dull; on the other hand, the characters of the
5 people who were associated with all those events are spellbinding. As a result, I have always been captivated by the character of Mary, Queen of Scots. I can relate to her because of her resemblance to people I know personally—not that I know any royalty, but I do know
10 many people who, like Mary, have struggled with the tangled and knotted circumstances of their own lives.

Born on December 8, 1542, Mary became a queen six days later when her father, James V of Scotland, died. In 1558 she was sent to France. Surrounded
15 by the indulgence and intrigue of the French court, this naïve teenage girl found her new life exotic and thrilling. She learned to play the lute, to write poetry, to ride a horse, to handle a falcon, and to flirt and titter and make herself the center of attention. At
20 just sixteen, she was joined in marriage to a young man named Francis, who became King of France the following year.

Yet Mary rapidly shifted from wife to widow: Francis died suddenly, and a year later Mary sailed to
25 Scotland, ready to play her role as Queen. She landed in an alien world. She was accustomed to play and pleasure, but Scotland was dour, grave, and patriarchal. For the first time in her life, Mary was antagonized merely because she was a woman. Across the border
30 in England, her cousin Elizabeth I had faced the same dilemma, yet had responded by adopting the aggressive attitudes of a King. Mary did not know how to follow her cousin's example: in France, she had been accepted as a young, beautiful woman and had
35 used her femininity to get what she wanted. The Scots would have none of this. They insisted that she marry to the advantage of the country's future and they chose Henry Stuart, Earl of Darnley, as Mary's consort. The union was a disaster.
40 Darnley was a churl and a boor. Selfish, spoiled, and arrogant, he treated Mary abominably. His only redeeming quality was his status as a potential heir to the English throne should Elizabeth never marry, a possibility which seemed increasingly likely. Mary
45 ignored him as much as possible, although the "union" did produce a son. She found her comfort elsewhere, if the rumors of the time are to be believed. There was Davide Rizzio, an Italian musician with whom Mary appeared to have a close relationship and who was
50 found stabbed to death: the rumor was that Darnley had murdered Rizzio in a jealous rage. The scandal shook Scotland, but worse was to come.

James Hepburn, the Earl of Bothwell, was quite the opposite of the effete Darnley: bearded, rough, and
55 full of vigor, he swept Mary off her feet. In February 1567, Darnley fell ill and was recuperating in a house at Kirk O'Field. One night, Mary visited him before going out to an evening wedding with friends. Some hours later, Kirk O'Field exploded in flames. Darnley
60 was killed in the incident—although his body was found not in the ruins but in the gardens of the house, not burned by the explosion but smothered to death instead. In April of that year, Bothwell was put on trial for the murder of Darnley, but was acquitted. Then in
65 June, Bothwell "abducted" Mary; it was later claimed that they had married. Scotland was outraged, and raised an army to track the refugees down. Although Bothwell evaded his pursuers, Mary was captured and her son was taken from her. Shortly afterwards,
70 she escaped to England and demanded the protection of Elizabeth, who promptly imprisoned her—for her own good, one might say. For the next eighteen years, Mary's presence in England was a threat to Elizabeth's reign. Eventually, Mary was tried for treason and
75 executed at Fotheringay Castle.

She entered the execution chamber, faced the witnesses, and removed her black outer dress to reveal her scarlet petticoats, perhaps as a last act of defiance. The axe was swung twice before her head was severed
80 from her body. The executioner then raised up her head by its golden hair, which turned out to be a wig intended to hide Mary's short gray crop. Beneath her skirts, her little Skye terrier was discovered, cowering but refusing to leave her side.
85 For me, this is what history is about. Mary may have been a bit on the profligate side, but she was a woman determined to live her life to the fullest— to be herself, to refuse to conform. Many of her contemporaries were glad to be rid of her, no doubt.
90 Then again, most of them are forgotten, but Mary is not.

30. The passage as a whole can best be described as

(A) an appreciative account of a historical figure's private life
(B) a polemic directed against abstruse historical writing
(C) a comparison of aristocratic lifestyles in sixteenth-century Europe
(D) an impartial summary of a political leader's ideology
(E) a record of titillating yet inconsequential gossip from an earlier era

31. Based on the information in the first paragraph, the author of the passage would most likely enjoy

(A) a timeline that presents the development of technologies used in naval warfare
(B) a biography of Napoleon that focuses mainly on Napoleon's psychology and personality
(C) a detailed analysis of the ideological conflicts behind the Protestant Reformation
(D) a survey of the works of fiction and poetry written by American colonists
(E) a lecture about a politician's efforts to unify two territories in the Middle East

32. In lines 17-19 ("She learned . . . attention"), the author lists

(A) talents that alienated Mary from her immediate family in Scotland
(B) achievements that would prove useful upon Mary's departure from France
(C) accomplishments that teenagers today should hold in high regard
(D) Mary's activities and attainments at the French court
(E) signs of Mary's seldom-acknowledged artistic ingenuity

33. It can be inferred that Mary "sailed to Scotland" (lines 24-25) as the result of

(A) the outbreak of hostilities between England and France
(B) the unanticipated death of her first husband
(C) a conspiracy against the French ruling elite
(D) a new marriage proposal that won her approval
(E) the unusual expectations of the Scottish court

34. Lines 28-36 ("For the . . . this") suggest which of the following about Mary?

(A) She had been indifferent to issues of governance during her early years, but became more proactive after relocating to Scotland.
(B) She had been adored by her husband Francis, yet was greeted with disdain and contempt by her Scottish acquaintances.
(C) She had enjoyed almost unlimited freedom during her childhood, and rebelled against the austere lifestyle of the Scottish elite.
(D) She revered her cousin Elizabeth, and was dismayed by her inability to emulate the young queen.
(E) She had been admired as an accomplished woman in France, whereas in Scotland she was regarded with much less esteem.

35. Mary's marriage to "Henry Stuart, Earl of Darnley" (line 38) can best be described as

(A) undertaken without public approval
(B) tumultuous yet ultimately rewarding
(C) motivated by political calculations
(D) symptomatic of larger social problems
(E) reflective of Mary's trusting nature

36. In line 45, the author puts the word "union" in quotations in order to indicate that

(A) marriages in the sixteenth century were remarkably different from the marital unions enacted today
(B) Darnley bore the sole responsibility for the failure of his marriage to Mary
(C) Mary and Darnley's interactions were unlike the harmony normally expected in marriage
(D) authorities in England and France did not regard Mary's marriage to Darnley as valid
(E) Mary was willing to openly criticize her marriage when she appeared in public

37. The passage suggests that Mary was infatuated with "James Hepburn, the Earl of Bothwell" (line 53) because Bothwell

(A) "evaded his pursuers" during his liaison with Mary (line 68)
(B) was remarkably dissimilar to "the effete Darnley" (line 54)
(C) pledged his assistance after Mary "escaped to England" (line 70)
(D) accepted Mary's "close relationship" with Davide Rizzio (line 49)
(E) was a "potential heir" to the English throne (lines 42-43)

38. The statement in lines 69-74 ("Shortly afterwards . . . reign") suggests that Elizabeth may have prolonged Mary's imprisonment because Mary was

(A) an intellectual adversary
(B) an insufferable egotist
(C) a reckless demagogue
(D) a prominent libertine
(E) a political liability

39. In line 80, "raised up" most nearly means

(A) lifted
(B) celebrated
(C) ascended
(D) exalted
(E) redeemed

40. Lines 76-84 ("She entered . . . side") make prominent use of

   (A) extended metaphors that explain Mary's state of anxiety
   (B) shifts in perspective that generate empathy for Mary's enemies
   (C) vivid details that help the reader to visualize Mary's execution
   (D) literary allusions that construe Mary as a tragic heroine
   (E) sensory descriptions that indicate the justice of Mary's fate

41. In the final paragraph, the author expresses approval of Mary, Queen of Scots because Mary

   (A) adhered to a stricter code of ethics than any of her peers
   (B) lived her life in a proactive and autonomous manner
   (C) permanently altered perceptions of women in England
   (D) was unaware of how her contemporaries perceived her
   (E) undermined the reputations of her political enemies

Answer Key: PART 3

Part 3

24/41 = 60%

PASSAGE 1

1. B
2. A
3. B
4. E
5. D
6. B
7. D
8. A
9. C

PASSAGE 3

18. B
19. C
20. A
21. E
22. D
23. E
24. B
25. A
26. E
27. B
28. C
29. D

PASSAGE 2

10. D
11. C
12. A
13. C
14. B
15. C
16. E
17. A

PASSAGE 4

30. A
31. B
32. D
33. B
34. E
35. C
36. C
37. B
38. E
39. A
40. C
41. B

Need an answer explained? Send the page number and the question number to **info@ilexpublications.com**, and we will send you a full analysis and explanation.

Post-Test Analysis

This post-test analysis is essential if you want to see an improvement on your next test. Possible reasons for errors on the four passages in this section are listed here. Place check marks next to the types of errors that pertain to you, or write your own types of errors in the blank spaces.

LONG READING PASSAGE 1:   **# Correct:** _3_   **# Wrong:** _6_   **# Unanswered:** _____

◇ Did not understand the questions or answers
◇ Did not understand the line references
◇ Read too much or too little around the line references
◇ Did not create effective margin answers
◇ Did not use process of elimination
◇ Could not find evidence to answer the questions
◇ Could not choose between two possible answers
◇ Could not comprehend the topic of the passage
◇ Interpreted the passage rather than using evidence
Other: _____

LONG READING PASSAGE 2:   **# Correct:** _6_   **# Wrong:** _2_   **# Unanswered:** _____

◇ Did not understand the questions or answers
◇ Did not understand the line references
◇ Read too much or too little around the line references
◇ Did not create effective margin answers
◇ Did not use process of elimination
◇ Could not find evidence to answer the questions
◇ Could not choose between two possible answers
◇ Could not comprehend the topic of the passage
◇ Interpreted the passage rather than using evidence
◇ Other: _____

> **Use this form** to better analyze your performance. If you don't understand why you made errors, there is no way that you can correct them!

LONG READING PASSAGE 3:   **# Correct:** _7_   **# Wrong:** _5_   **# Unanswered:** _____

◇ Did not understand the questions or answers
◇ Did not understand the line references
◇ Read too much or too little around the line references
◇ Did not create effective margin answers
◇ Did not use process of elimination
◇ Could not find evidence to answer the questions
◇ Could not choose between two possible answers
◇ Could not comprehend the topic of the passage
◇ Interpreted the passage rather than using evidence
Other: _____

LONG READING PASSAGE 4:   **# Correct:** _8_   **# Wrong:** _4_   **# Unanswered:** _____

◇ Did not understand the questions or answers
◇ Did not understand the line references
◇ Read too much or too little around the line references
◇ Did not create effective margin answers
◇ Did not use process of elimination
◇ Could not find evidence to answer the questions
◇ Could not choose between two possible answers
◇ Could not comprehend the topic of the passage
◇ Interpreted the passage rather than using evidence
Other: _____

Part 4

Questions 1-8 are based on the following passage.

*In the following passage, adapted from an essay
written in 2013, the author considers a large festival
that takes place in his hometown of Domfront,
France.*

It is hard to believe that way back, in the Middle
Ages, the little town of Domfront was of some
importance to this part of Normandy - and to France
Line as a whole, too. Kings, English and French, fought
5   each other here. Nobles squabbled over land and
power. Pilgrims on their way to Mont St. Michel
rested from their journeys here. Domfront was alive
and bustling and rich. Then, in 1608, following a plan
to diminish the power of the nobility in France and
10   appoint Louis XIV as absolute monarch, the castle
was pulled down. The old town then declined into a
sleepy state that has lasted for almost five
hundred years.

There are some fairly notable events that break
15   the monotony, of course. A small market of about
nine stalls offering everything from fresh vegetables
to almost-fresh fish to flowers, cheeses, and female
underwear appears on the Place General de Gaulle
for four hours every Friday morning. This is the high
20   point of the week for the elderly – of whom there
are many in the town: young people cannot wait to
escape to the large cities elsewhere. For the most
part, the streets of contemporary Domfront are
quiet and still.
25   However, biennially, the dull and dusty sheets
of history are thrown off and Domfront relives
its glorious past. The oldest part of town, which
lies between the castle ruins and St. Julien's
Church, bursts with banners and coats of arms. The
30   distinctive rhythms of sackbuts and horns, shawms
and pipes, timbrels and drums, rebecs and other
stringed instruments rebound against the ancient
stone walls. White tented stalls fill the Place St
Julien, the original market square of Domfront. The
35   stall holders, dressed in the comfortable smocks
and cloaks of the Middle Ages, sell hand-dyed
clothes, leather belts and shoes, spices, candies, and
biscuits made from recipes handed down through
the generations. Up at the Castle, the horses, draped
40   and saddled, wait to be mounted by knights in armor
for the jousting tournament. Archery butts are put
in place, so that today's Robin Hoods can show
their prowess. Wrestlers grapple and roll across the
greensward. Beyond the narrow passageways that
45   lead off the central square, in the cobbled courtyards
that once were the houses of the rich, trestles groan
with pitchers of mead and local pear cider for the
hot and thirsty, who are now seeking relief from the
bustle of the main square. A flock of horned sheep
50   wanders through the alleys, watched over by a sharp-
eyed collie and a shepherd with his crook.

In another courtyard, a troubadour entertains. Flag
throwers, jugglers, and tumblers draw gasps from
the onlookers.
55   This is the weekend of Le Mediaeval, and it
takes place during the first weekend of August. The
festivities begin on Friday afternoon, when all the
parking places in the old town are cleared of vehicles
and replaced by tented stalls. The castle gates are
60   ceremonially closed and then reopened. For the next
two days, the visitor will have to pay to enter, if the
events there are to be viewed. Later that evening
there is a banquet for the great and the good of the
town, provided that they have paid for their tickets
65   and that they arrive in medieval garb. This feast takes
place under canvas. The meal can be both drafty
and damp: August in Domfront is often heralded by
thunderstorms.

The next morning Le Mediaeval officially
70   begins with a parade of the market stallholders, led
by mounted knights and halberdiers in costume.
The mayor welcomes the procession with a speech
and, to great fanfare, declares the opening of the
celebrations. There is a crowd of locals and tourists,
75   many of them dressed in period costume, and the
attendance swells as the weekend proceeds. The old
city is alive again, as it was in days long past. By
Sunday afternoon the streets are packed and noisy.

The festival officially ends at 6:00 pm on
80   Sunday. By early Monday morning, the old town
has returned to normal. No flags, no music, no
stalls remain - even the horse droppings have been
removed. The streets are silent and empty again.
Domfront sleeps for another two years. Until then,
85   the past is another country only glimpsed in dreams.

1. The primary purpose of the passage is to

   (A) memorialize an important period of
   prosperity in French history
   (B) question the importance of a celebration for
   the residents of a town
   (C) describe a festival that evokes the spirit of a
   city's history
   (D) propose that festivals similar to La
   Mediaeval be instituted in other towns
   (E) criticize the events that take place during a
   town-wide festival

2. In the first paragraph, the author suggests that
   Domfront is no longer the busy town it once was
   because of

   (A) economic depression
   (B) architectural renovation
   (C) artistic innovation
   (D) political upheaval
   (E) excessive pilgrimage

3. In context, the phrase "rested from" in line 7 is closest in meaning to

(A) interrupted
(B) revitalized
(C) ended
(D) abandoned
(E) began

4. The items mentioned in lines 16-18 ("offering everything…underwear") can best be described as

(A) incomplete
(B) obscure
(C) comprehensive
(D) eclectic
(E) tedious

5. The phrase "dull and dusty sheets of history" in lines 25-26 refers to

(A) a halcyon period of life in Domfront
(B) the lengthy dormancy of Domfront
(C) the upheaval that took place in 1608
(D) Domfront before the rule of Louis XIV
(E) the spirited party held biennially in Domfront

6. Lines 29-54 ("The distinctive …onlookers") serve primarily to describe

(A) a reenactment of Domfront's glory days
(B) an accurate retelling of the history of Domfront
(C) one stop for a traveling Renaissance fair
(D) a scale model of Domfront's current market
(E) an homage paid to the kings of the past

7. The feast described in the fourth paragraph differs from the parade described in the fifth paragraph in that

(A) the feast requires all of its participants to appear in medieval dress, whereas the parade enforces no such stricture
(B) the feast is a uniformly depressing affair, whereas the parade is an unprecedented expression of joy
(C) the feast puts considerable financial strain on Domfront, whereas the parade requires little expenditure
(D) the feast has always taken place during inclement weather, whereas the parade has never been interrupted by thunderstorms
(E) the feast is open exclusively to Domfront residents, whereas the parade permits the attendance of tourists and other outsiders

8. The phrase in lines 82-83 ("even the…removed") is used to

(A) highlight the pride with which the people of Domfront regard their city
(B) suggest that La Mediaeval produces very little litter during its celebration
(C) emphasize the extent to which evidence of the celebration is erased from Domfront
(D) discuss the high degree of waste that is produced during La Mediaeval
(E) describe just how quiet Domfront is on a regular day without celebration

Questions 9-21 are based on the following passage.

This passage was written by an amateur historian. In the account that follows, the author describes entertainment showcases known as the "Promenade Concerts" or "Proms".

Originally, a Promenade Concert was an open-air event. People strolled through one of the many pleasure gardens of London while an orchestra
Line played music in the background. Then in 1895,
5 Robert Newman, wishing to establish a larger audience for classical music, created a different kind of "Prom": Proms moved indoors, with both areas of seating and galleries where people could stand to listen. There was always a fairly low entrance fee
10 to encourage a less wealthy audience, and there was also an emphasis on the more popular classical works in order to attract those who knew little of classical music. Newman was an entrepreneur, not a musician, and he put the choice of program in the hands of Sir
15 Henry Wood, possibly the most important English conductor of the time. After all, Wood promoted the work of vibrant new composers such as Delius, Richard Strauss, and Ralph Vaughan Williams.
When Newman went bankrupt, the patronage
20 of what had become known as the "Sir Henry Wood Promenade Concerts" at the Queen's Hall was taken over by others until, eventually, these events were put in the financial care of the BBC. When the Queen's Hall was destroyed in the Blitz of 1941, the
25 Proms were moved to The Royal Albert Hall. This auditorium was—and still is—an ideal space for the Proms, in terms of both capacity and acoustics. There are tiers of seats for those who have the money for them and the ability to book in advance, but these
30 concertgoers need to be quick, since the tickets sell out almost within a week of being offered on sale. Admission to the various galleries on each level of the Hall is only available on the day of performance; however, the cost here is minimal, because in the
35 galleries one has to stand throughout the concert. Equally cheap and again only available on the day of performance is the standing arena just in front of the orchestra's platform. The people who jam themselves into this space are known as "Promenaders," for they
40 are the link with the origins of this annual event, which runs for eight weeks in the summer.
Yet thanks to the BBC, you can enjoy the Proms for nothing. Every performance is broadcast on the radio and many of them are televised, sometimes
45 live but often recorded for airing at a later date. The UK is the only country in the world that has such an organization as the BBC, and it is an immensely lucky country in this respect: the BBC is, quite possibly, the single greatest supporter of the arts in
50 the world. Under this network's guidance, the Proms have grown and evolved. In addition to the great

orchestral events in the Albert Hall, chamber concerts are held in the nearby Cadogan Hall, and various Proms in the Park take place in many different cities
55 across the country. All of these showcases are free, all are managed and financed by the BBC. The scope of the music that is performed each season has gradually widened, until now the concerts range from full performances of six-hour-long operas by Wagner to
60 nights devoted to the works of Stephen Sondheim and Rodgers and Hammerstein, not to mention Hollywood musicals and the theme songs of British and American films.
Some musical purists have scoffed at this
65 inclusiveness, presuming that melodies designed to accompany westerns or love stories have nothing to do with classical music. These elitists forget that Tchaikovsky, Verdi, Puccini, and Mozart—though not able to pen film scores for quite obvious reasons
70 —actually did for the popular entertainments of their times what the composers of film scores do for today's movies. Everyone can recognize the opening bars of Beethoven's Fifth Symphony, and everyone can recognize the music that John Barry devised for
75 the haunting theme of *Out of Africa*, or the raucous trumpets of the James Bond films. Hitchcock thrillers would not grip and involve their audiences quite so much without the scores of Bernard Hermann. It is not difficult to imagine Beethoven and Verdi nodding
80 with approval. Music snobs should also remember Robert Newman's original intentions when he started the Proms back in 1895. Although some may have qualms about an afternoon performance devoted to the music of *Doctor Who*, today's children can
85 only benefit from the realization that a real orchestra making music can be just as exciting as the electric throbbing of an iTunes playlist.
The Proms are now part of the UK's national heritage: nowhere is this more evident than in the
90 Royal Albert Hall on the last night of the Proms every year. Flags are waved furiously by the Promenaders, balloons are let loose, streamers are thrown into the orchestra. "Rule Britannia" is sung with gusto and so is "You'll Never Walk Alone", and these songs
95 echo through London and through the entire country, projected far and wide on large screens. Behind the orchestra, on a pedestal, is the laurel-wreathed bust of Sir Henry Wood, smiling benignly. Nobody remembers Robert Newman, though.

9. The primary purpose of the passage is to

(A) describe the evolution of an important aspect of modern British culture
(B) provide capsule biographies of the most influential British composers
(C) persuade concert and performance venues to lower their admissions fees
(D) cast doubt on the judgment of today's most respected scholars of music
(E) encourage tourists to visit the UK and attend the Prom performances

10. As described in the first paragraph, the original "Proms"

(A) were democratic in nature, whereas Newman's Proms catered to the aristocracy
(B) drew on international music, whereas Newman's Proms featured only English composers
(C) were open-air events, whereas Newman's Proms took place indoors
(D) involved a full orchestra, whereas Newman's Proms focused on prominent soloists
(E) alienated non-specialists, whereas Newman's proms pleased novice musicians

11. In the context of lines 19-23 ("When Newman . . . BBC"), the BBC is significant because it

(A) helped Britain maintain civil order during the Blitz of 1941
(B) eventually assumed the patronage of the Promenade Concerts
(C) outlawed the collection of admissions fees at musical events
(D) gathered the funds necessary to build The Royal Albert Hall
(E) played a pivotal role in lifting Robert Newman out of bankruptcy

12. The word "cheap" in line 36 most nearly means

(A) shoddy
(B) opportunistic
(C) miserly
(D) inexpensive
(E) easy

13. The first two paragraphs of the passage function primarily to

(A) provide historical background for a feature of British life that persists to the present day
(B) emphasize the character traits that musical conductors need in order to prosper
(C) specify the artistic properties of the new musical compositions that Wood promoted
(D) point out the importance of collaboration in the creation of new musical events
(E) delineate the class distinctions that caused tension at the earliest Prom performances

14. According to the passage, it is now possible to "enjoy the Proms for nothing" (lines 42-43) because

(A) the Proms offer complimentary admission to all visitors from abroad
(B) music from the Proms is featured every night on British news programs
(C) transportation costs plummet during the eight weeks of the summer Proms
(D) the Albert Hall follows a free admission policy for all of its events
(E) the BBC airs the performances, allowing them to reach a large audience

15. In lines 45-50 ("The UK . . . world"), the author's tone is one of

(A) disbelief
(B) ambivalence
(C) admiration
(D) haughtiness
(E) conciliation

16. Which of the following best summarizes the evolution of the Proms, as described in the third paragraph?

(A) The Proms have gradually alienated many once-loyal listeners.
(B) The Proms have begun to systematically reject traditional music.
(C) The Proms are now dominated by the music of American composers.
(D) The finances of the Proms continue to experience periods of instability.
(E) The repertoire of the Proms has expanded over time.

17. In the fourth paragraph, the author mentions "musical purists" (line 64) in order to

(A) promote respectful debate among scholars of music
(B) raise doubts about the reader's own musical knowledge
(C) preface an empirical analysis of musical tastes
(D) introduce a viewpoint that he argues against at length
(E) undermine the reputations of several famous composers

18. On the basis of lines 83-84, the author appears to regard an "afternoon performance devoted to the music of *Doctor Who*" as

(A) a potentially rewarding experience for certain concert-goers
(B) a spectacle designed to insult and alienate the traditional audience for the Proms
(C) an indication of the astonishing versatility of British composers
(D) a financial liability for the current organizers of the Proms
(E) an increasingly important tradition for certain citizens of the UK

19. In line 91, the word "furiously" most nearly means

(A) angrily
(B) energetically
(C) provocatively
(D) desperately
(E) unreasonably

20. In lines 93-94, "Rule Britannia" and "You'll Never Walk Alone" are mentioned as

(A) examples of popular songs that musical elitists regularly deride
(B) compositions that were especially revered by Sir Henry Wood
(C) selections that are performed enthusiastically on the final night of the Proms
(D) works that only the most dexterous musicians can perform
(E) songs that have been memorized by the majority of British civilians

21. The situation described in lines 96-99 ("Behind the . . . though") most closely resembles which of the following?

(A) An innovative philosopher successfully predicts advances in technology that occur 150 years in the future.
(B) A young attorney creates his own firm, and uses unconventional tactics to win cases against more established lawyers.
(C) A soccer player leads his team to a series of stunning victories, but refuses to grant interviews and press conferences.
(D) A poet spends decades pursuing public recognition, but is only acknowledged as a major author in his old age.
(E) Two accomplished chemists form a biomedical company, but only one of these individuals is commemorated at the firm's 50th anniversary celebration.

Questions 22-29 are based on the following passage.

Excerpted from a short story, the passage below focuses on an antique shop in a suburb of London. Ms. Bernard, a middle-aged woman, is the owner of the shop; Peter, who is newly retired, has been appointed to look after the premises in her absence.

The stained sign above the shop read "Vintage Wares and Bric-a-Brac."

Peter stood in the road and peered through the
Line grubby window of the little shop. The display—if
5 "display" were the correct word—presented two
wilting wicker chairs, a series of mouldering copper
pans, and a small table covered with a grubby cloth,
on which had been placed a statuette of a half-draped
woman. With her 1920s bobbed haircut, this statuette
10 woman sat on what might have been a tree stump
and looked over her shoulder with a rather coy smile.
There were also the corpses of several flies.

Peter thought back to the day before. Ms. Bernard,
the owner, had suggested that he might like to "look
15 after" the shop, which had been closed in the three
months since the last assistant had walked out. "We
were away, at the villa in Majorca," Ms. Bernard
had explained, "when your do-nothing predecessor
disappeared. No possibility of sorting out the situation.
20 And then, of course, we had the Convention to attend
in the United States. Mark and I are exhausted. It
is almost Christmas and there are so many charity
dinners and events we have to attend, and no chance
to do anything about the shop. Then Mark thought of
25 you. He thought it might be something to occupy you
since you've had nothing to do since your retirement."

Ms. Bernard had then paused and added, "And it
would help us out."

Peter had digested both the insult and the petition
30 and had thanked Ms. Bernard for her thoughtfulness.

He took the keys from his pocket, unlocked the
door, entered the shop, gingerly picked his way over a
splintered straw basket from which spilled a small herd
of brass horses, and stared around. The shop stared
35 back at him, sullen and silent. It held the chill of dust
and neglect. On a long table in the center of the floor
were piled, higgledy-piggledy, incomplete sets of dull
brandy glasses and wine carafes, odd china beer mugs,
a pair of ancient leather boxing gloves, and a hideous,
40 biliously pink china cake stand. In one corner stood
a tilted, dilapidated, and much-stained table with a
round top: in another, a tumble of grimy bronze salvers
spilled from a sad carver chair. Against a wall keeled
a grubby chaise longue that seemed to have only three
45 legs. On it, tattered paperbacks sprawled, mingled
with a couple of large atlases and a heap of mold-eaten
stationery.

Out of habit, Peter began to stack the books
into alphabetically ordered piles on the floor. This task
50 took some time. Then he turned his attention to

the stationery. One by one, each paper was picked
up, shaken out, folded neatly, and placed, color
coordinated, on top of the books. Peter regarded the
neat stack. "Well, it's a start," he said aloud, and went
55 home for lunch.

He returned that afternoon with an electric kettle,
a mop and pail, several sponges, pieces of flannelette,
and a very large can of polish. He wore a pair of denim
overalls. He heated some water and filled the pail.
60 "I think," he proclaimed, as if to an unseen spirit,
"you need a little care and a lot of love."

There was the sound of what might have been a
sigh, but perhaps was only the falling of dust.

It was Christmas Eve when Ms. Bernard returned.
65 She stood in the road and gazed at the glistening
window display. Along the bottom of the draped
scarlet backdrop, a row of gleaming brass figure
flashed in the reflected light. A small vintage lamp sat
proudly on the deeply glowing small round table.
70 Center stage, raised high on a dark green base, a
marble statue of a beautiful young woman was poised.
She gave the impression of having been interrupted
from a reverie, and she turned her head coquettishly
towards the glass window, as if promising delight to
75 anyone who entered the portal of the shop.

Ms. Bernard turned to Peter, a worried look on her
face. "Where on earth did you find these things? You
didn't go out and buy them, I hope, because I cannot
afford that kind of a bill. You'll have to take them
80 back."

Peter gave her a steady look. "You don't like it?"

"Well, of course, it is a very striking display. But
really, Peter, how much did you spend on all this?"

"I don't know. How much is a can of Mr. Clean?"
85 "You mean that all these things were in the shop
already?"

Peter nodded. "It's just a question of
acknowledging their true nature, a little care and a lot
of love."
90 Ms. Bernard entered the shop and looked around,
a grin spreading across her face. The shop grinned
back.

22. The phrase "if 'display' were the correct word"
(lines 4-5) is best characterized as

(A) an ambiguous expression
(B) a whimsical allusion
(C) a qualifying statement
(D) a broad generalization
(E) a surprising rebuttal

23. In lines 29-30 ("Peter had . . . thoughtfulness"), it can be inferred that Peter is

(A) flattered by Ms. Bernard's trust, but fearful that he will disappoint her
(B) irked by Ms. Bernard's callousness, yet eager to earn her good regard
(C) offended by Ms. Bernard's assumptions, but willing to assist her nonetheless
(D) satisfied with Ms. Bernard's offer, yet reluctant to ask for future responsibilities
(E) dismayed by Ms. Bernard's words, but anxious not to reveal his chagrin

24. The description of the store's contents in lines 31-47 ("He took . . . stationery") primarily conveys

(A) chaos and unpredictability
(B) artistry and idiosyncrasy
(C) sorrow and alienation
(D) skepticism and confusion
(E) dinginess and neglect

25. In lines 48-53, the description of Peter's actions ("Out of . . . books") functions primarily to

(A) establish Peter's intolerance of any form of disorder
(B) illustrate Peter's conscientious and meticulous way of working
(C) praise Peter's refined sense of color an proportion
(D) allude to the standards of cleanliness instituted by Ms. Bernard
(E) suggest the level of attention that the rest of the antique shop will require

26. The expression "There was the sound of what might have been a sigh" (lines 62-63) is an example of which of the following rhetorical devices?

(A) Personification
(B) Euphemism
(C) Understatement
(D) Anecdote
(E) Digression

27. By using phrases such as "scarlet backdrop" (line 67) and "Center stage" (line 70), the author compares Peter's window display to

(A) a menagerie
(B) a museum
(C) a theater
(D) a schoolhouse
(E) a landscape vista

28. In line 71, "poised" is closest in meaning to

(A) refined
(B) expectant
(C) proper
(D) shaped
(E) positioned

29. Which of the following most closely resembles the situation described in lines 76-92 ("Ms. Bernard . . . back")?

(A) The owner of a small clothing store builds up a loyal clientele, yet sees his profits decline due to competition with larger establishments.
(B) A young art student is entrusted with his teacher's studio, and uses found objects to create inexpensive sculptures that win praise from his mentors.
(C) A successful lawyer returns to his hometown to attend a family reunion, and finds that many of his distant relatives have changed radically from when he last saw them.
(D) A chef in an expensive restaurant creates dishes that are routinely praised by food critics, but that many casual diners regard as unappetizing.
(E) A newly-elected mayor announces a major project to beautify his town, yet modifies this plan when he realizes that few of the residents will lend assistance.

Questions 30-42 are based on the following passage.

This passage is taken from a biographical study of British Renaissance playwrights and poets.

We know little about Shakespeare's home life: it seems to have been relatively staid, safe, and comfortable, almost domestic. The same cannot
Line be said of the everyday affairs of Shakespeare's
5 greatest rival, dramatist Christopher Marlowe. Like a teenage superstar, Marlowe was flashy and rough and physical, lived on the edge, was determined to try everything. Open-minded and often outspoken on the most dangerous topics of his day, particularly sex and
10 religion, he ruffled feathers and caused offense to many; he was condemned as a heretic, magician, duellist, tobacco user, rake-hell. "Kit" Marlowe put up the Elizabethan equivalent of two fingers in response laughed, and roistered on, a rebellious, dangerous
15 firebrand. Every generation has one. It is easy to forget that, had "Kit" Marlowe's life not been terminated by a dagger through his right eye during a brawl at a notorious Cheapside inn, it is possible that the artistic fame of Christopher Marlowe might have totally
20 eclipsed that of William Shakespeare.

Christopher Marlowe worked for a theatre that competed with Shakespeare's home troupe. Shakespeare wrote for Richard Burbage, an actor of subtlety who could reveal the complexities of human
25 relationships. Marlowe wrote for Edward Alleyn, who was physical and virile in performance and could express the world as Marlowe saw it: a world in which power was always the ultimate goal:

"Is it not passing brave to be a king, Techilles,
30 Usumcasane, and Theridimas?
Is it not passing brave to be a king
And ride in triumph through Persepolis?"

This is Tamburlaine the Great, the scourge of Asia, speaking to his generals in the Christopher Marlowe
35 play that bears his name. *Tamburlaine* was Marlowe's first smash hit. Audiences were shocked by the violence of the script, but loved the sheer ferocity and rampaging single-mindedness of the title character. In addition, Marlowe was the first playwright to
40 use blank verse, which is the poetic form that best approximates the rhythm of the English language itself, and audiences were thrilled by the directness and clarity of meaning in Marlowe's writing. Two plays soon followed *Tamburlaine*: *Edward II* and *The Jew*
45 *of Malta*, each one a precise portrayal of how power manifests itself through treachery, double-dealing, and other Machiavellian pursuits. The characters in these plays are egoistic, arrogant, brutal, and all doomed to die, yet these characters speak in verse that
50 makes us comprehend the divide between the physical necessities of survival in this earthly world and the

aspirations to spiritual grace that we are taught to value. This insight was revolutionary for an audience unprepared for the outspoken frankness of the
55 dialogue. Apparently, Marlowe was moving into very dangerous territory.

While "Christopher" Marlowe was the poet and playwright, "Kit" Marlowe was most probably a spy for Queen Elizabeth's government, picked out for
60 this role during his studies at Cambridge University. We have no direct proof, just convincing innuendos and hints that point in this direction. Marlowe made secret trips into hostile Europe, was captured but was soon released. Somebody clearly was protecting
65 him, and his aggressive attitude was a useful cover. If you appear so definitely to be a blustering rebel, eventually, people just shake their heads, laugh fondly, and decide not to take you too seriously. In any case, "Kit" Marlowe, spy, discovered first-hand how power
70 really works and used this knowledge in his work as a playwright.

He drew on this background most coherently in *Doctor Faustus*, a drama in which the central character makes a bargain with the devil's agent, Mephistophilis:
75 Faustus gives his soul in return for power and praise in this world for two dozen years. The play is a coruscating, satiric reflection on the place of Man in the order of things, and the script's scope swings from high tragedy to lowest farce and back again. The first
80 stage appearance of *Doctor Faustus* was electrifying: spectators claimed that there were real devils onstage amongst the actors. Marlowe would have thrown his head back in laughter had he heard this. He didn't, though, for he was dead and buried six months before
85 the play was first staged

Kit, the spy, and Christopher, the poet and dramatist, both looked for truth and reason behind the posturing surfaces of two different worlds. Shakespeare and other poets of the time explained
90 discord and disorientation as the conflict between the physical demands of the Body and the spiritual aspirations of the Soul. Marlowe wasn't the kind of man to accept this poetical, philosophical concept. He went unerringly for the jugular. Early
95 in his adventures, Faustus summons the fiendish Mephistophilis and questions him: "How is it that thou art out of Hell?" Mephistophilis replies, "Why, this is Hell, nor are we out of it."

In this, both "Kit" and "Christopher" would
100 have been in complete agreement. No other poet of the period would have had the nerve to make such a heretical and subversive statement, on or off the Elizabethan stage. The death of Christopher Marlowe was mourned by all those who worked in the
105 Elizabethan theatre: still, his demise must have been a relief to the authorities of England.

30. In the first paragraph, the author indicates that Shakespeare's lifestyle was

(A) fairly unexciting, whereas Marlowe's was distinguished by controversy and conflict
(B) marked by material comfort, whereas Marlowe endured periods of poverty
(C) generally antisocial, whereas Marlowe had a multitude of friends and colleagues
(D) thoroughly austere, whereas Marlowe's was astonishing in its opulence
(E) psychologically uninteresting, whereas Marlowe's still baffles biographers

31. The author of the passage compares Marlowe to a "teenage superstar" (line 6) most likely in order to

(A) summarize the opinions of Marlowe's enemies
(B) emphasize Marlowe's daring and showy temperament
(C) excuse Marlowe's most controversial behavior
(D) criticize Marlowe's irresponsible and egocentric decisions
(E) provide the reader with a specific allusion to popular culture

32. In describing Marlowe as a "heretic, magician, duellist" (lines 11-12) the author is most likely paraphrasing

(A) contemporary scholars of Renaissance literature
(B) magic specialists and ghost hunters from centuries ago
(C) a character from one of Marlowe's most renowned plays
(D) participants in a few of Marlowe's illicit pursuits
(E) critical observers who lived in the same era as Marlowe

33. It can be inferred from lines 15-20 ("It is . . . Shakespeare") that Marlowe's death

(A) was symptomatic of a rise in criminal activity that plagued England during Marlowe's lifetime
(B) prevented Marlowe from winning the public recognition that had been denied him so often
(C) brought to a sudden end a playwriting career that could have been even more remarkable than Shakespeare's
(D) was long regarded as an inevitable consequence of Marlowe's recklessness and irresponsibility
(E) stunned and dismayed even Marlowe's staunchest competitors in the theatre

34. In context, the "world as Marlowe saw it" (line 27) was

(A) motivated largely by issues of power
(B) inhospitable to men of true artistic genius
(C) marred by shortsighted self-interest
(D) controlled solely by those who are brave
(E) impressed by violence and anarchy

35. As described in lines 35-47 ("*Tamburlaine* was . . . pursuits"), Marlowe was the first British playwright to

(A) analyze the complex relationship between power and politics
(B) compose his dramas in a particularly lucid form of verse
(C) include sensationally violent sequences in the majority of his scenes
(D) simultaneously inspire controversy and admiration
(E) write his manuscripts using arcane English words

36. In line 59, "picked out" most nearly means

(A) criticized
(B) antagonized
(C) separated
(D) transplanted
(E) selected

37. In lines 61-65 ("We have . . . cover") the author indicates that Marlowe's identity as a spy is

(A) plausible according to the available evidence, but is still not possible to verify definitively
(B) a logical conclusion, yet has been disproven by intensive research
(C) fascinating to amateur historians, but has never been the subject of a full-length study
(D) one of Marlowe's own fabrications, and was maintained by Marlowe's admirers
(E) intriguing to present-day readers, but was of little interest to Marlowe's contemporaries

38. By drawing a distinction between "Christopher" Marlowe and "Kit" Marlowe in lines 57-71, the author indicates which of the following?

(A) Marlowe's works have puzzled archivists, and were at one point classified under two different names.
(B) Marlowe wanted to keep his artistic and governmental pursuits separate, and consequently developed a pseudonym.
(C) Marlowe's plays are of uneven quality, and a few of his weakest have been attributed to a second writer.
(D) Marlowe can be understood to have two different personas, one artistic and the other political.
(E) Marlowe developed a firm beliefs about governance, though these ideas were incompatible with the tenets of his plays.

39. As described in lines 72-76 ("He drew . . . years"), *Doctor Faustus* is a play that

(A) ultimately rejects superstition and encourages worldly pragmatism
(B) was influenced by Marlowe's firsthand experience of how power operates
(C) was lambasted by many as a tacit endorsement of atheism
(D) is impossible to understand without knowledge of Marlowe's espionage career
(E) includes multiple allusions to political events that Marlowe had witnessed

40. The situation described in lines 79-85 ("The first . . . staged") most closely resembles which of the following?

(A) A motivational speaker is too busy to attend an important conference, and sends a competent subordinate in her place.
(B) A reclusive painter becomes the subject of a museum retrospective, but refuses to attend the exhibition's opening reception.
(C) A composer changes his artistic principles radically, and shuns live performances in order to focus on studio work.
(D) A celebrated director and his actors revise much of the dialogue of a screenplay after the death of its author.
(E) An architect creates blueprints for a daring new skyscraper, yet does not live to oversee the construction of the building itself.

41. In line 89, the author mentions "Shakespeare and other poets of the time" in order to

(A) introduce an interpretation of reality that conflicts with Marlowe's ideas
(B) establish Shakespeare's superiority as a poetic stylist
(C) demonstrate how Shakespeare's worldview was inherently flawed
(D) compare Faustus to a few of Shakespeare's tragic protagonists
(E) cast doubt on Marlowe's awareness of philosophical principles

42. It can be inferred that Marlowe's death was a "relief to the authorities of England" (line 106) on account of his

(A) "open-minded and often outspoken" personality (line 8)
(B) disregard for the "complexities of human relationships" (lines 24-25)
(C) "physical and virile" self-image (line 26)
(D) taste for both "high tragedy" and "lowest farce" (line 79)
(E) disdain for "poetical, philosophical" concepts (line 93)

Questions 43-51 are based on the following passage.

The following passage is extracted from an essay by a director of Shakespearean plays. Here, the author discusses the preservation of The Complete Works by William Shakespeare.

It is a moot point, perhaps, but the probability
is that if Shakespeare were alive, well, and talented
today, he would not be writing for the theatre. It seems
Line clear—from the few facts that we can verify of his rise
5 from the relative rags of the butcher trade to a secure
niche of retirement within the Upper Middle class of
Elizabethan society—that he had a sharp nose to sniff
out where the money was among the trend-setters of
his age. Finding the Earl of Southampton and keeping
10 him happy (and generous) with the odd dedication,
doing a favor for the Earl's mother by acting as a
kind of tutor to her son (and attempting to steer him
towards an acceptable marriage), cozying up to the
Burbage family and providing them with hit material
15 for the most fashionable show in town (in a new and
specially-designed setting, which they named, rather
naïvely, "The Theatre"), not to mention being at least
on nodding terms with Royalty: all this conjures a
figure that is highly recognizable in the twenty-first
20 century. We would know Shakespeare today from
appearances (probably bare-chested) on the covers of
teen magazines, from sets on late night talk shows,
chatting about his latest album and the possibility of
graciously doing Hollywood a favor. We would read
25 about the clubs to which he goes, how many love
affairs he is having, the number of times he has been
seen with members of European Royal families or has
been invited to the White House.

What we would not have are The Complete
30 Works. It seems clear that, were Shakespeare living
today, he would have precious little time to send a
Tweet, let alone write plays for the theatre and for
posterity.

Well, we do have The Complete Works, may the
35 Muses be praised! However, it should be noted that
we would not have access to them had it not been for
the enthusiasm of Hemminge and Condell, a couple
of seventeenth-century character actors whose role
in the preservation of Shakespeare's works is made
40 all the more significant by the challenges they faced:
although publishing was well-established by the
seventeenth century, plays were ephemeral. Essays,
treatises, the King James edition of the Bible, poetry:
all of these flowed into the market. But not plays. The
45 theatre was not regarded as a Temple of Literature;
rather, it was regarded as "seditious" by the authorities
and was required to remain inconspicuous. More
practically, the theatre companies did not want their
box-office successes published for fear they would be
50 used by rival companies. The laws of copyright did
not exist, as yet. The only dramatist to have his plays

printed was Ben Jonson, and he, personally, oversaw
the printing process, ensuring accurate versions and
not travesties of what he had actually written.
55 So, after the death of Shakespeare, when
Hemminge and Condell decided to publish his works,
it was an act of "homage" to the memory of a fellow
member of the theatrical profession whom they had
revered. It was not an easy task, that's for sure. They
60 had to try to find the original, hand-written scripts that
had been literally dashed off by Shakespeare in the
urgency of achieving his deadlines, each document
full of changes of mind and crossing-outs and notes
scribbled in the margins. Where these were not
65 available, then the individual actors' scripts had to
be unearthed—and these would have to be pieced
together laboriously, for an actor never received a full
version of the play: just a couple of hand-scribbled
lists of his own lines, each speech preceded by a cue.
70 Re-writes during rehearsal may have been noted on the
edges of the pages—or not, as the case may be. (Film
scripts are nothing new, in this respect). Sometimes,
there were no originals to be found and Hemminge and
Condell had to rely on the memories of the surviving
75 members of their theatre company, memories that were
not always trustworthy. In addition, and in contrast
to the procedures of the conscientious Jonson, no one
really edited or supervised the printers at work. Thus,
all kinds of errors could be—and often were—made.
80 The fact that these errors occurred has been
grist to the mill for the thousands of Shakespearean
scholars in the centuries that followed, not to mention
for theatre directors, film makers, critics, historians,
poets, and philosophers. Thus it was that the great
85 Shakespeare Industry was set in motion by two of
his greatest fans, an industry based on cut-and-paste
recollections of verses that are revered today as the
paragon of literary excellence. And yet this industry
generates millions of dollars a year all round the
90 world. Shakespeare himself would probably have
approved of this—although he might be regretting that
he is no longer around to benefit

43. The author mentions that Shakespeare "had a
sharp nose to sniff out where the money was"
(lines 7-8) primarily in order to

(A) criticize a celebrity for being overly
materialistic
(B) provide a detail about a dramatist that is later
refuted
(C) trivialize the worldly pursuits of a playwright
(D) suggest that the theatre was a lucrative
profession
(E) explain how a personality managed to better
his lot in life

44. The tone in lines 30-33 ("It seems . . . posterity.") can best be described as

(A) informative
(B) laudatory
(C) outraged
(D) ironic
(E) disinterested

45. The word "Well" (line 34) serves to

(A) transition from a hypothetical situation to an actuality
(B) repudiate a remark about the theater from earlier in the passage
(C) add humor to an otherwise earnest proposition
(D) emphasize Shakespeare's apparent health
(E) expose a shocking truth about the power of muses

46. The words "More practically" (lines 47-48) serve to differentiate between

(A) the secrecy that surrounds the theatre and the accuracy of the printing press in its incipience
(B) a box office failure and a commercial success
(C) a playwright's adherence to conventional ideas and his desire to protect his intellectual property
(D) a playwright's religious convictions and his competitive drive
(E) what is regarded as ethical and what is ostensibly beneficial

47. All of the following are mentioned as reasons for why "it was not an easy task" (line 59) EXCEPT

(A) failure to keep notes
(B) failure to remember lines
(C) frequent edits
(D) difficulty of the language
(E) scribbled writing

48. The phrase "dashed off" in line 61 most nearly means

(A) ran
(B) deleted
(C) punctuated
(D) written
(E) crossed out

49. The phrase "Where these were not available" (lines 64-65) refers to

(A) "The Complete Works" (lines 29-30)
(B) "character actors" (line 38)
(C) "his works" (line 58)
(D) "hand-written scripts" (line 60)
(E) "actors' scripts" (line 65)

50. In the final paragraph the author suggests that

(A) Shakespearean verse, as is known today, may be different from its original form
(B) Shakespeare's plays were not written by Shakespeare
(C) Shakespeare would disapprove of the commercialization of his works
(D) Scholars are profiting enormously from errors in Shakespearean verse
(E) Shakespeare's fans are disappointed by the inaccuracies in his verses

51. The primary purpose of this passage is to

(A) document the role of playwrights in the history of publishing
(B) assign credit to its rightful place as it relates to the preservation of a body of work
(C) argue against the excessive importance attached to a well-known historical figure
(D) cast doubt as to the true author of a well-known body of work
(E) promote a greater appreciation of classical literature and its historical relevance

Answer Key: PART 4

Part 4

PASSAGE 1

1. C
2. D
3. A
4. D
5. B
6. A
7. A
8. C

PASSAGE 2

9. A
10. C
11. B
12. D
13. A
14. E
15. C
16. E
17. D
18. A
19. B
20. C
21. E

PASSAGE 3

22. C
23. C
24. E
25. B
26. A
27. C
28. E
29. B

PASSAGE 4

30. A
31. B
32. E
33. C
34. A
35. B
36. E
37. A
38. D
39. B
40. E
41. A
42. A

PASSAGE 5

43. E
44. D
45. A
46. E
47. D
48. D
49. D
50. A
51. B

Need an answer explained? Send the page number and the
question number to **info@ilexpublications.com**, and we
will send you a full analysis and explanation.

Post-Test Analysis

This post-test analysis is essential if you want to see an improvement on your next test. Possible reasons for errors on the five passages in this section are listed here. Place check marks next to the types of errors that pertain to you, or write your own types of errors in the blank spaces.

LONG READING PASSAGE 1:   # Correct: _____   # Wrong: _____   # Unanswered: _____

- ◇   Did not understand the questions or answers
- ◇   Did not understand the line references
- ◇   Read too much or too little around the line references
- ◇   Did not create effective margin answers
- ◇   Did not use process of elimination
- ◇   Could not find evidence to answer the questions
- ◇   Could not choose between two possible answers
- ◇   Could not comprehend the topic of the passage
- ◇   Interpreted the passage rather than using evidence

Other: _____

LONG READING PASSAGE 2:   # Correct: _____   # Wrong: _____   # Unanswered: _____

- ◇   Did not understand the questions or answers
- ◇   Did not understand the line references
- ◇   Read too much or too little around the line references
- ◇   Did not create effective margin answers
- ◇   Did not use process of elimination
- ◇   Could not find evidence to answer the questions
- ◇   Could not choose between two possible answers
- ◇   Could not comprehend the topic of the passage
- ◇   Interpreted the passage rather than using evidence
- ◇   Other: _____

> **Use this form** to better analyze your performance. If you don't understand why you made errors, there is no way that you can correct them!

LONG READING PASSAGE 3:   # Correct: _____   # Wrong: _____   # Unanswered: _____

- ◇   Did not understand the questions or answers
- ◇   Did not understand the line references
- ◇   Read too much or too little around the line references
- ◇   Did not create effective margin answers
- ◇   Did not use process of elimination
- ◇   Could not find evidence to answer the questions
- ◇   Could not choose between two possible answers
- ◇   Could not comprehend the topic of the passage
- ◇   Interpreted the passage rather than using evidence

Other: _____

Continue to the next page.

Post-Test Analysis

This post-test analysis is essential if you want to see an improvement on your next test. Possible reasons for errors on the five passages in this section are listed here. Place check marks next to the types of errors that pertain to you, or write your own types of errors in the blank spaces.

LONG READING PASSAGE 4:   **# Correct:** _____   **# Wrong:** _____   **# Unanswered:** _____

   ◇   Did not understand the questions or answers
   ◇   Did not understand the line references
   ◇   Read too much or too little around the line references
   ◇   Did not create effective margin answers
   ◇   Did not use process of elimination
   ◇   Could not find evidence to answer the questions
   ◇   Could not choose between two possible answers
   ◇   Could not comprehend the topic of the passage
   ◇   Interpreted the passage rather than using evidence
Other: _____

> **Use this form** to better analyze your performance. If you don't understand why you made errors, there is no way that you can correct them!

LONG READING PASSAGE 5:   **# Correct:** _____   **# Wrong:** _____   **# Unanswered:** _____

   ◇   Did not understand the questions or answers
   ◇   Did not understand the line references
   ◇   Read too much or too little around the line references
   ◇   Did not create effective margin answers
   ◇   Did not use process of elimination
   ◇   Could not find evidence to answer the questions
   ◇   Could not choose between two possible answers
   ◇   Could not comprehend the topic of the passage
   ◇   Interpreted the passage rather than using evidence
   ◇   Other: _____

Part 5

Questions 1-8 are based on the following passage.

*The following passage, excerpted from an article
written in 2013, outlines a scandal that brought about
great change in 1960s Britain.*

If you want to know why the decade beginning
in 1960 had such a transformative effect on British
life, then you need to begin with a dramatic trial
Line in the High Court of London in 1963. Performing
5　in what turned out to be both a tragedy and a farce
was a free-ranging cast of surprising characters.
The plot-line here would seem, on the surface, to be
tacky even by the standards of one of Russ Meyer's
Hollywood films, which were popular at the time and
10　consisted mainly of starlets in bikinis doing nothing
other than posing and posturing self-importantly
around a swimming pool.
　　The "Profumo Affair," as the case in question
was called, even opened with a swimming pool.
15　This infamous pool lay in the English countryside
on the outskirts of London at the Cliveden Estate,
which belonged to Lord Astor, a backstage political
tsar. At said pool, weekend guests from the ruling
class mingled with visitors to whom they, the elite,
20　had no apparent public connection. Among others,
John Profumo, the British Minister of War, was a
frequent guest at Cliveden. Despite being married,
Profumo allegedly became more sociable with the
charming young hostesses at this getaway than
25　might be acceptable. In the busy, strained life that is
government, such peccadillos might well occur. All
perfectly harmless, or so it would seem.
　　Even back in the sixties, private lives had a
way of becoming public property. At the time of
30　her short-lived dalliance with Profumo, a Cliveden
visitor named Miss Keeler had an almighty—and
rather public—bust-up with an ex-boyfriend. This
ex-boyfriend had been angered by Miss Keeler's
dalliance with a suspected Soviet spy. Miss Keeler,
35　it seemed, along with another girl, Miss Davies,
was living at the flat of the organizer of the
Cliveden parties. The press publicly questioned
why the Minister of War should have connections
to an alleged spy. Foolishly, Profumo stated to
40　Parliament that he had never met the man and that
"no impropriety had occurred." Still, the press can
follow a scent, emitting more noise and radiating
more intensity than a pack of foxhounds: journalists
discovered that both Miss Keeler and Miss Davies
45　had been paid to catch the attention of the Soviet
ambassador. Reports escalated in imaginative
speculation and lurid innuendo, which climaxed
in two spectacular events: John Profumo admitted
that he had perjured himself and was immediately
50　expelled from office, while an anonymous party
planner was put on trial for providing more than
charming hostesses to a corrupted Cliveden.

The trial was a press sensation. For the first
time, it seemed, the corruption of the ruling class
55　of England was being exposed. During the trial,
the details of the parties emerged as Lord Astor
and the others under interrogation spluttered
indignantly at the suggestions of corruption, denying
any knowledge of what was going on. The girls
60　were insouciant in their responses. When the Lord
High Justice stared balefully at Miss Davies and
declaimed, "Do you know that Lord Astor has denied
any knowledge of you at all?" she grinned cheerfully
and replied, "Well, he *would* say that, wouldn't he?"
65　The country nearly erupted in applause. The
game was up for the old regime at last. As a result
of this trial, the career of an able but naïve politician
was ended, a Prime Minister resigned "on the
grounds of ill health," the ruling political party
70　lost the next election, the freedom of the press was
encouraged to a level never before seen in Britain,
and, most importantly, the existing class system was
upended. England would never be the same again, no
longer fettered by what "the great and the good" of
75　the nobility decided. From 1963 onward, at any rate,
the youth of Britain felt free to "let it all hang out"
and bring on the novel idea of "Swinging London."

1.　The author's primary purpose in writing this
　　passage is to

(A) describe the ways that 1960s British films
　　accurately depicted everyday life
(B) present a new theory to account for the
　　political struggles in 1960s foreign affairs
(C) examine the various ways the lower classes
　　were able to move up in rank in 1960s
　　Britain
(D) explain an incident that contributed to the
　　social changes in 1960s Britain
(E) persuade the reader that sensationalism in
　　the media adversely affects the possibility
　　of a fair trial

2.　The author mentions "a free-ranging cast of
　　surprising characters" (line 6) in reference to

(A) a typical scene in a controversial Russ
　　Meyer film script
(B) the popular fiction genres of the 1960s,
　　especially farce and legal drama
(C) the people whose lives were negatively
　　affected by social change in 1960s Britain
(D) the participants in the Profumo Affair Trial
(E) the privileges of the judges and those in
　　power in 1960s England

3. The author compares the "infamous pool" at Cliveden (line 15) to

   (A) pools in popular movies that demonstrate other contemporary changes in morality
   (B) fountains at garden parties that recall earlier times of social upheaval
   (C) lakes in the countryside that were hollowed out using modern technology
   (D) ponds in cities that have become too polluted by industry for civilian use
   (E) swimming pools normally used by film stars to relax after their ordeals on set

4. In context, the last sentence of the second paragraph ("All perfectly… seem") makes use of

   (A) digression
   (B) parody
   (C) metaphor
   (D) irony
   (E) exaggeration

5. In the third paragraph, the details about Miss Keeler and Miss Davies primarily function as

   (A) specific instances of the new casual attitude in 1960s British lifestyles
   (B) rebuttals of the anticipated argument that the government worked to maintain the status quo
   (C) important reminders of global political contingencies that modern readers may not consider
   (D) background information about the event that would eventually end Profumo's career
   (E) emotional appeals to the reader which encourage respect for the division between public and private life

6. The author uses the phrase "a pack of foxhounds" (line 43) to emphasize the

   (A) frenetic confusion of investigators heading off in different directions
   (B) subtle cunning of undercover reporters searching for informants
   (C) ferocious desire of the media to find the truth in spite of a flimsy lead
   (D) underlying motivation of the judicial system to expose deleterious political dealings
   (E) superficial fervor that masks a hidden apathy in media reporting

7. The description of the trial in the fourth paragraph (lines 53-64) presents an image of the nobility as

   (A) justified and ignorant, while the common people appear resourceful and conniving
   (B) deceitful and pompous, while the common people appear candid and poised
   (C) righteous and unyielding, while the common people appear sympathetic and gregarious
   (D) unified and resilient, while the common people appear capricious and histrionic
   (E) condescending and vapid, while the common people appear intelligent and willful

8. Which of the following situations is most analogous to the impact of the Profumo Affair as described in the last paragraph?

   (A) An overbearing business tycoon is arrested for embezzlement, and his company falls into the hands of a younger executive with a more liberal management style.
   (B) A disgruntled university student discovers that his professor has plagiarized numerous articles, so he reports the crime anonymously and encourages the college administration to fire the professor.
   (C) An incompetent but well-meaning social worker assists a released convict in finding a job and starting a new life.
   (D) A federal legislator reconsiders his position on key social issues and switches parties to better serve the changing needs of his constituents.
   (E) A young working woman convinces a noble gentleman to marry her so that she can spread populist principles through his elitist family.

Questions 9-17 are based on the following passage.

This passage, adapted from a 2013 essay about Shakespeare's theatre, was written by a professor of literature.

The film *Shakespeare in Love* is a witty and relatively accurate representation of what most people know about the theatre of Shakespearean and Elizabethan times. The Globe, as it is shown
Line
5 in the film, recalls the images that many of us saw as school children. Many of us remember, too, that the theatre was not regarded in a favorable light by the authorities, who took every opportunity to prevent performances. Drama was seen as an
10 encouragement to immorality and sedition against the state – not to mention that the playhouses were seen as extremely unhealthy places to visit in those periods when England experienced outbreaks of the plague. *Shakespeare in Love* also
15 contains less familiar facts, which perhaps only the Shakespeare cognoscenti would recognize: the rivalry between the different theatre companies, and the rivalry between Shakespeare and Burbage over a somewhat rudimentary version of the "Dark Lady" of
20 Shakespeare's sonnets. Scholars of English Literature will smile at the thumbnail sketch of John Webster, who is portrayed as an enthusiastic and salacious teenager hanging around the fringes of the Globe. These asides and touches are essential to the film's
25 success, for they persuade the audience to believe in what it is seeing, though there is one element of the story which, in fact, could never have happened: the use of a real woman in the role of Juliet.

It seems bizarre to us today that, in
30 Shakespeare's England, young boys could perform in public but no woman could. There was no law that denied women the right to appear; however, the poor players who strutted and fretted their time upon the stage were regarded as little more than vagabonds
35 with extremely low codes of morality. For this reason, although it was never stated, it was clear that an audience would not have accepted the presence of women on stage. Although some protestations were aired on the subject of boys appearing in the
40 supposedly louche company of players, this was the only way to learn the craft of acting. Thus, the boys were apprentices in the theatre, in the same way that they might have been accepted into one of the more formal and traditional guilds that had existed in
45 England since the Middle Ages.

Some commentators appear to think that the use of boys to play female roles stems in part from the ecclesiastical tradition of choirboys. The treble voice of a young boy is, musically, both thrilling and
50 chilling. Thrilling, because the soaring, pure notes a young boy can produce echo the intention of church music: to bring the listener to a closer relationship to God. However, this singing is also chilling precisely because it is so pure. It has none of the warmer
55 timbre which marks the female voice. If vocal pitch were the only reason for employing boy actors, it surely must follow that many of the boy players were doomed to a limited career: once the voice cracked – as is assumed in *Shakespeare in Love* – the boy's
60 career was over, yet this was not the case at all.

Theatre historians confuse Shakespeare's boy actors with members of the deliberately formed children's companies who performed clever literary plays by John Lyly, each script full of classical
65 allusions and relevant references to contemporary society. These child actors played at the enclosed Blackfriar's Theatre, before an audience made up of aristocrats and intellectuals. Nonetheless, the troupe's temporary popularity affected the earnings of the
70 theatres on the South Bank of the Thames. These child actors are the "little eyeases" to which Hamlet refers: their vogue did not last long and they are now a footnote in the history of the theatre.

As in the guilds, the typical boy apprentice
75 joined an acting company around the age of twelve. Playing pages and messengers and sundry other roles, he learned the craft of acting and developed his skills. We like to think that these boys reached the roles of Viola, Portia, and Rosalind because of talent.
80 However, if we look carefully, we can see how the female roles are crafted to the boy actor's limitations. In the comedies, for example, notice how quickly Rosalind and Viola are whisked into masculine clothing – so much more familiar for a young man.

85 So, we do not have to worry about the poor boy whose voice, apparently, broke just before he was about to speak his first line as Juliet. We do not know his name. It could have been a boy called Alex Cooke, but it would be fitting if it turned out to
90 be another boy actor, Joseph Taylor. When Richard Burbage retired from the stage, it was Taylor who took over all the great actor's roles. Not bad for one who started as "a little eyeas."

9. In the sentences "The Globe...performances" (lines 4-9), the author assumes that

(A) his audience has more than a passing familiarity with the Shakespearean theatre
(B) the only readers interested in his essay will most likely be Shakespearean scholars
(C) the creators of *Shakespeare in Love* are among the readers of this essay
(D) *Shakespeare in Love* takes too many liberties with its London setting
(E) most readers are ignorant of the conditions of life in Shakespeare's time

10. In line 16, the word "cognoscenti" most nearly means

    (A) authorities
    (B) affiliates
    (C) students
    (D) directors
    (E) secret society

11. The author claims that "these asides and touches are essential to the film's success" (lines 24-25) most likely because

    (A) the contemporary audience for Shakespeare's work is interested primarily in his biography
    (B) the filmmakers altered the details of Shakespeare's early life in order to satisfy a modern audience
    (C) they convince the audience that it is watching a fairly accurate re-creation of Shakespeare's milieu
    (D) *Shakespeare in Love* is intended not only to teach about Shakespeare's life, but also to entertain
    (E) Shakespearean characters are based on stereotypes that are still recognized today

12. Unlike the aspects of *Shakespeare in Love* described in lines 14-23, the "use of a real woman" (lines 27-28) is

    (A) an oversight made by the director
    (B) a blatant factual inaccuracy
    (C) a re-creation of an actual performance
    (D) a little-known piece of Shakespearean trivia
    (E) an insufficient solution to an artistic problem

13. According to the first paragraph, the authorities wanted to prevent performances at the Globe Theatre for all of the following reasons EXCEPT:

    (A) the promotion of disreputable behavior
    (B) unsanitary conditions that led to contagion
    (C) the vulnerability of theater-goers to infectious disease
    (D) the emboldening of insurrectionists
    (E) the prominent use of female actors

14. The second paragraph suggests that women did not act on stage because

    (A) it was uncommon for women to work side-by-side with men at the time
    (B) female roles were already filled by young male actors whom audiences adored
    (C) acting was an unprofitable profession and not many women were in need of income
    (D) laws were enacted to bar women from the debauchery of acting
    (E) theatergoers did not want to see women in such degraded circumstances

15. In context, the contrast between the "pure" voice and the "warmer" voice (lines 53-55) is best described as

    (A) pious vs. scandalous
    (B) fearful vs. assured
    (C) terrifying vs. passionate
    (D) haunting vs. comforting
    (E) assertive vs. faint

16. The author explains that the situation described in lines 55-60 ("If vocal…all") was caused by

    (A) mistaking Shakespearean boy actors for children acting in literary plays
    (B) the low survival rate of records documenting the theatre history of the Elizabethan Era
    (C) the absence of interest in the female roles in Shakespeare's plays
    (D) fundamental uncertainty about the laws dictating who could act in theatre at the time
    (E) playwright John Lyly drawing Shakespeare's boy actors to his own theatre

17. It can be assumed that the "female roles" in line 81 were

    (A) meant to be appreciated by readers and theater-goers centuries later
    (B) designed with the preferences and capabilities of Shakespearean boy actors in mind
    (C) a relative rarity in Shakespeare's body of work
    (D) lacking in psychological complexity compared to Shakespeare's roles for men
    (E) consciously parodied by competing playwrights such as John Lyly

Questions 18-29 are based on the following passage.

The following passage is taken from a short story set in present-day France.

"What a lovely way to celebrate! Thank you
so much," said Catherine, as she eased the car onto
the highway. "I have to hand it to you Parisians: you
Line   certainly know how to prepare food."
5   Edmond smiled modestly. "It has a good
reputation, that restaurant. And its wine cellar is
renowned."
        "You seemed to be quite familiar with it. I guess
the French train their children from an early age."
10   "Certainly. A good wine is excellent for the
digestion. And it has a calming effect, very necessary
when you are driving."
        She gave him an ironic glance. "Thank you so for
that. You can always get out and walk."
15   Edmond's eyes twinkled. "Certainly not. I like
your driving, even if, being English, you sometimes
forget which side of the road you should be on."
        The road passed through the forest, now tinged
with the russet shades of autumn. For the most part,
20   the trees crowded the roadside, yet every now and
then there was a small open space, rather rutted in the
places where drivers had stopped for recreation. In
some of these clearings, there were stacks of logs from
felled trees.
25   "The French are so cheeky!" Catherine exclaimed.
"Imagine churning up the forest like that. Look at
those women over there: they just stopped their car in
the middle of the glade and went to pick mushrooms.
In England, those women would be prosecuted for
30   Trespassing and Theft. I wonder what the owner would
say."
        "Nothing, I should think," remarked Edmond.
"Actually, I am one of the owners."
        Catherine shot him a surprised glance. Edmond
35   explained: "The national forests belong to the people
of France. It is the right of every French citizen to
forage in the forests and gather food and kindling from
the forest floor. Of course, the state attempts to look
after the forest: thus the tree-felling and the protection
40   of forest animals when hunting is no longer in season.
Otherwise, we can do anything we like there."
        "Hunting, like English hunting? With hounds
and horses?" Catherine was suddenly impassioned.
"I hate hunting. It should be banned outright. There
45   is no excuse for allowing a cruel and disgusting sport
indulged in by the idle rich—unspeakable activities in
pursuit of uneatable animals."
        "There speaks the modern Englishwoman, who
thinks that her food, perfectly shaped and washed and
50   packaged, appears miraculously at the supermarket,
ready to go into the microwave. We French know that
good food is food taken straight from the earth and not
frozen and given a sell-by date. We take food seriously.

Our forests are full of edible produce: truffles,
55   mushrooms, herbs, and of course deer and wild boar."
        "So, you believe that hunting is acceptable?"
        "Certainly, if the aim is to hunt food for the table.
The English don't believe that. They hunt for sport, for
the thrill of the chase."
60   "No, hunting in any form is wrong. Chasing
terrified animals with hounds ready to rip their prey to
pieces—it's barbaric."
        Edmond shrugged his shoulders. "I agree. No
Frenchman would touch venison brought down that
65   way. Here, hunting an animal is not akin to murder.
In France, the hounds chase the deer because the deer
are agile runners—it is what makes their meat so lean
and healthy—and the dogs' role is to direct the deer
to where it can be brought down by the huntsman,
70   cleanly and efficiently, so that it will be acceptable for
eating."
        "That is no way to treat any wild animal."
        "All animals were originally wild. You think
that because some animals are reared on farms, those
75   animals they are somehow house-trained; that's why
you call them 'domestic' animals. Little calves and
piglets are so sweet."
        "Well, so they are."
        "Oh, yes, sweet for three months, and then you
80   take them to the slaughterhouse. How else would you
get your ham and veal?"
        Catherine's face flushed. She felt confused.
        There was silence in the car for the next few
kilometers, then Edmond said, "Turn into the next
85   Aire, please."
        "What's an 'Aire'?" Catherine asked crossly. "You
mean a parking area?"
        "Yes, a parking area," he answered gently.
        The car bumped over a grass verge and into a
90   small clearing. Catherine switched off the engine. The
stillness now seemed tremendous, universal. Catherine
gazed out the window. A red squirrel darted across the
grass and scampered up the gnarled trunk of an ancient
oak. Then, once again, silence settled all around.
95   Catherine leaned back in her seat. "It is beautiful."
she said at last. "Your forest is so beautiful."

18. The episode presented in the passage is best
     described as a

     (A) disappointment experienced by two
          colleagues
     (B) conclusive negotiation about a controversial
          issue
     (C) drive through a countryside that is rapidly
          being destroyed
     (D) dispute between two impetuous individuals
     (E) lively debate about a divisive topic

19. The tone of the statement in lines 15-17 ("I like . . . on") can be best described as

   (A) sentimental
   (B) ambivalent
   (C) diffident
   (D) resigned
   (E) wry

20. Catherine's remarks to Edmond in lines 25-31 ("The French . . . say") indicate her assumption that forests are

   (A) areas where access is denied to all but a few small groups of visitors
   (B) pristine landscapes unworthy of human exploration
   (C) public domains that are endangered by industrialization
   (D) private properties that should be protected from intruders
   (E) wildlife reservations that are protected from all forms of contamination

21. The tone of Catherine's statements in lines 44-47 ("I hate . . . animals") can be best described as

   (A) nonplussed
   (B) incendiary
   (C) indignant
   (D) suspicious
   (E) hyperbolic

22. According to Edmond, the central contrast between the English and the French in lines 48-55 ("There speaks . . . boar") is best described in which terms?

   (A) Aggression versus indifference
   (B) Presumption versus appreciation
   (C) Uniformity versus diversity
   (D) Diffidence versus certainty
   (E) Civilization versus disorder

23. What does the use of the words "terrified" (line 61) and "barbaric" (line 62) indicate about Catherine?

   (A) Her acceptance of current hunting practices
   (B) Her unwavering objection to animal domestication
   (C) Her visceral opposition to hunting
   (D) Her cultural elitism regarding a popular sport
   (E) Her passionate dedication to animal safety

24. Edmond's words in lines 65-71 ("Here, hunting . . . eating") imply that hunting is acceptable when it

   (A) achieves its ends without causing undue suffering
   (B) dismantles preconceived notions about ancient methods
   (C) overturns accepted practices in pursuit of new advantages
   (D) presents its participants with an aesthetically pleasing spectacle
   (E) expresses the values of resourcefulness and collaboration

25. In context, the word "sweet" in line 77 most likely conveys

   (A) sarcasm
   (B) exasperation
   (C) zealotry
   (D) vitriol
   (E) understatement

26. The "silence in the car for the next few kilometers" (lines 83-84) is most likely indicates Catherine's

   (A) passivity
   (B) conviction
   (C) fanaticism
   (D) naïveté
   (E) vexation

27. In lines 90-94 ("The stillness . . . around"), the atmosphere in the clearing can best be described as

   (A) placid
   (B) gloomy
   (C) ominous
   (D) ebullient
   (E) triumphant

28. In line 91, "universal" most nearly means

(A) fundamental
(B) capacious
(C) general
(D) encompassing
(E) inclusive

29. Catherine and Edmond would most likely agree on which point about hunting?

(A) It is an expression of cruelty regardless of the circumstances.
(B) It is likely to have unfortunate effects on woodland ecosystems.
(C) It is tolerable when implemented within strict legal limits.
(D) It is deplorable when undertaken purely for sport.
(E) It is regarded as a purely recreational activity in both France and England.

Questions 30-39 are based on the following passage.

This passage is from a 2013 book by a professor of Renaissance politics and culture.

In 1553, Henri IV of France was born in Navarre. He was a Catholic, but converted to Protestantism (or became a Huguenot, as French Protestants are
Line called). His early life was not without incident. At the
5 age of nineteen, he married the young aristocrat Marguerite de Valois, thus aligning himself with a prominent Catholic family. The marriage was meant to create harmony between the Catholics and the Huguenot factions, although the fact that the groom
10 had to stand outside the doors of Notre Dame while the marriage ceremony was conducted within the church hardly suggests that this reconciling intention was fulfilled.

The couple's honeymoon was quite short.
15 Exactly six days after the marriage, the streets of Paris were filled with a mob of French Catholics seeking to assassinate Huguenots, an event later known as the Massacre of Saint Bartholomew. The search was not confined to the streets alone, for we
20 have an account written by Marguerite herself describing how her bedroom was burst into by a young soldier fleeing the massacre. He flung himself upon her bed, begging for protection but, to the horror of the nineteen year-old girl, was dragged
25 away by Catholic soldiers and slain. Henri himself was imprisoned. He was not killed, for he was not only the King of Navarre but also a "Prince of the Blood" and, therefore, the heir to the French throne —unless a miracle occurred and the present king
30 produced a male heir. Not long after his incarceration, Henri escaped to Tours; it was from there that he embarked on what history calls "the French wars of religion." His aims were to secure the throne and to stabilize the country. He achieved these aims when,
35 in 1589, he entered Paris as the newly-Catholic Henri IV; playing on his new convictions, he delivered the comment *"Paris vaut bien une messe."* This, translated, is "Paris is well worth a Mass," although some later—perhaps rather cynical—commentators
40 have suggested that a more accurate translation might be "Paris is rather a mess."

Actually, those who feel that the second translation might be more accurate could have a better insight into what Henri meant by his remark.
45 The whole of France was disjointed, disunited and decaying—more than a bit of a mess, in fact. Henri set about making changes to the country of which he was finally monarch, and these changes were widespread and long-lasting. He enacted the Edict of
50 Nantes in 1598, thus allowing Protestants to worship as they wished and encouraging religious tolerance. He had roads built across the country—long, straight, and direct roads, lined with the trees for shade (his

idea) which are now regarded by all visitors to the
55 country as endemically French. He had the French Royal Palace built, but made sure that his chief minister, Sully, demolished many of the castles in the countryside of France. These time-honored structures had provided shelter for the old nobility
60 and had left whole communities in poverty and at the beck and call of those in provincial power. He began to create the bureaucracy which is so beloved by the French (Henri's system was later completely overhauled by Napoleon, another French ruler
65 who thought that things in France were a mess and needed a re-working). Above all, Henri was one of the more popular leaders of France, a country not generally noted for its reverence for those in power. He understood what actually mattered to people,
70 declaring that "I want there to be no peasant in my kingdom so poor that he is unable to have a chicken in his pot every Sunday." This is one of the sayings most remembered by the French: it is in all the school textbooks. Determined to live daringly, he had three
75 wives (not at the same time) and lots of love affairs (some of them probably at the same time). He had six children, ensuring that his line would endure. Above all, he spoke the language of ordinary people. He is reported as having said of himself, *"On a le*
80 *bras armé et le cul sur la selle*."* No wonder he was popular.

Still, you cannot please all the people all of the time. His death came in 1610. He was assassinated by Francois Ravouillac, who was a Catholic: old
85 convictions die hard. He left behind his son, Louis XIII, who was still a child. Thus it was that Henri's third wife, Marie de Medici, acted as regent until Louis grew old enough to take the reins. He, in turn, was followed by the resplendent Louis XIV and by a
90 period of French history that still dazzles. Yet, none of that would have occurred if, in 1589, Henri IV had not reined in his horse and looked down at the city he was about to enter and murmured, *"Paris vaut bien une messe"*—however we choose to translate it.

*"I rule with a weapon in my hand and my hindquarters in the saddle."

30. The primary purpose of the passage is to

(A) outline how French History is taught in schools
(B) explain the difference between Catholicism and Protestantism
(C) declare that marriage for political reasons will always fail
(D) correct misconceptions about the history of the French bureaucracy
(E) discuss the tumultuous career of a French icon

31. The author discusses Henri IV's marriage in lines 4-13 ("At the . . . fulfilled") in order to

    (A) explain the personal events that led to Henri IV's exile from the country
    (B) analyze the reasons behind the Catholic-Protestant rift
    (C) explain a religious fissure that influenced French society in the time of Henri IV
    (D) give a historical lesson about the childhood of the King of Navarre
    (E) highlight a commonly known fact about the everyday lives of French royalty

32. The author believes the second translation, "Paris is rather a mess" (line 41), was apt because at that time

    (A) the edict of Nantes was intolerant of any religious difference
    (B) Paris was in complete disarray both religiously and physically
    (C) Henri IV's marriage caused more controversy than accord
    (D) the original translation was grammatically incorrect
    (E) the phrase required too high an education for the commoners to understand

33. The discussion of Henri's changes in lines 46-66 ("Henri set . . . re-working") reflects Henri's belief that

    (A) Napoleon's bureaucracy needed a major overhaul
    (B) Protestants deserved to share power equally with Catholics
    (C) France's greatness should be reflected in its castles
    (D) the needs of the people should be addressed through proactive reforms
    (E) France should be decentralized with power handed back to the provinces

34. According to the second paragraph, Henri IV was responsible for reforms in all of the following areas EXCEPT

    (A) infrastructure
    (B) religion
    (C) the military
    (D) society
    (E) the government

35. The statement in lines 70-72 ("I want . . . Sunday") characterizes Henri IV as

    (A) a leader who understood what his people needed
    (B) a jovial king who enjoyed good food and many wives
    (C) a ruler who was out of touch with the realities of his nation
    (D) a monarch on the verge of being removed from power
    (E) a hedonist who irresponsibly spent his nation's wealth on luxuries

36. The parenthetical remarks in lines 75-76 serve primarily to

    (A) qualify a statement made earlier
    (B) mock the petty attitude of Henri IV
    (C) commiserate with the wives of the king
    (D) encourage research on a new topic
    (E) add humorous quips from the author

37. The primary purpose of the statement in French in lines 79-80 ("on a le . . . la selle") is to

    (A) describe the essence of a person's belief system
    (B) highlight the popularity of a political slogan
    (C) translate a description back into its original language
    (D) illustrate the way a monarch punished his enemies
    (E) mock a man for his crude choice of words

38. In context of the passage, the statement in lines 84-85 ("old convictions die hard") serves to

    (A) narrow the focus of an argument
    (B) criticize a religious group for its policy of intolerance
    (C) offer an alternate explanation for an infamous historical event
    (D) return to an idea raised earlier in the passage
    (E) underscore the need for further analysis

39. The overall tone of the passage is

    (A) remorseful
    (B) nostalgic
    (C) wry
    (D) admonishing
    (E) informative

Questions 40-48 are based on the following passage.

This passage is adapted from an essay in which the author is asked to teach in Africa and fundamentally change his way of living.

It is strange how life can change in an instant. As if it were only yesterday, I remember a time when life changed for me. For five years I had been teaching
Line in a small boarding school on Anglesey, a small
5 island separated from the mainland of Wales by two hundred yards of sea called the Menai Straits. The school was situated in the village known locally as Lanfair P.G. (Its full Welsh name is quite a bit longer and, while more accurate, both dreadfully hard to
10 remember and terribly difficult to pronounce.) The tourists from England still come every summer to visit this village with the longest name in the United Kingdom, but the school where I worked exists no more. Lack of pupils led to bankruptcy, so I was left
15 without a job and I seemed to have little likelihood, at my age, of quickly finding another. Despite advertising my availability as an educator, I failed to garner any positive replies. Then, early one morning, as I stood by the window of my small apartment
20 watching the mists over the Menai Straits slowly dissipating to reveal Mount Snowdon, Wales's most famous mountain, the phone rang.
"I am speaking to you from Malawi," announced a very English voice. I sighed with irritation. The last
25 thing I needed at that moment of my life was a prank phone call. "Malawi is the very small country about halfway down the eastern side of Africa."
"I know," I snapped. Then I paused. Was I picturing Malawi or Mozambique? Before I could
30 decide, the voice continued.
"I am the new Headmaster at the school here in Blantyre. I find that I am short of an English teacher. I saw your advertisement. Have you ever thought about teaching in Africa?"
35 The answer to that seemed fairly obvious to me. However, before I could think of a suitably dismissive riposte, I found myself agreeing to fax my qualifications. If everything proved suitable, I would be offered a post in Malawi within ten days.
40 In a daze, I put the phone down and, in the manner of the famous actress Meryl Streep in *Out of Africa*, murmured in an affected Danish accent, "I have a job in Arfreekah."
It was not until I was on the final leg of the
45 journey from Johannesburg to Blantyre, sitting in a cramped plane with "Air Malawi" stenciled in peeling paint on its tail, being buffeted by every swirling air current, looking down at the land below which seemed nothing but a featureless, uniform
50 brown, that the reality of what I was doing began to sink in. For a moment, I was in a panic. This was thousands of miles away from the comfortable

landscape of Lanfair P.G. The frail plane descended, bounced across the grassy landing strip and came
55 to a sudden halt outside a wooden building with a corrugated iron roof. Formalities were brief. Vainly looking for a familiar face, I followed the other passengers out of the shabby building.
It was not the warmth of the sun that caught my
60 attention first. Instead, the scent of Africa was most immediate. It is the smell of dung, the scent of the *jacaranda[1]*, the aroma of straw and dust, the waft of bananas in the flat woven baskets balanced on the heads of the women majestically walking in their
65 colorful draped cotton. All this melds intoxicatingly together to create an unforgettable perfume. It is the smell of warmth and life, and it sings like the faint songs that are always heard somewhere in the distance. The earth is not brown, but reddish, glowing
70 in the sun. There is a pulse in the air, not frenetic as in the cities of Europe nor gently and greenly soft as in the Welsh countryside: it is the slow steady beat of life unfolding in the measured rhythm of an earth that has been and will be here forever. I had been in
75 Africa for ten minutes and I felt already its embrace that seemed to whisper, "Forget the past. You are here now. Stay until you need to move on. We will always be here when you wish to return."
Such a strange yet familiar sensation! I felt the
80 tension in my chest fade. I picked up my suitcase and looked around. A few yards away sat a battered jeep. At the steering wheel sat a grinning Malawian, welcoming me. He waved me over.
"You are the new teacher?"
85 I nodded.
"Welcome to Malawi. You will be happy here."

1 A large flowering tree now common in Africa

40. The passage is best interpreted as an account of

(A) a man's adaptation to life on a new continent
(B) a teacher's experience of unavoidable circumstances
(C) an extreme life change with a pleasing outcome
(D) the impact of cultural exchange on a developing nation
(E) a man's apparent resentment of his home country

41. The word "garner" as used in line 18 most nearly means

(A) earn
(B) reward
(C) complete
(D) approve
(E) consolidate

42. The author snapped "I know" in line 28 most
likely because he

(A) was embarrassed that he had confused two
very different countries
(B) was insulted that someone thought he did
not know geography
(C) was irritated by what seemed to be a prank
phone call
(D) was angry that his original job had been
eliminated at the last minute
(E) was frustrated at the bizarre interruption of
his peaceful life

43. In context, the author's tone in lines 35-36 ("The
answer . . . me") can best be described as

(A) ecstatic
(B) snide
(C) disingenuous
(D) objective
(E) perplexed

44. The author claims that the answer was
"obvious" (line 35) most likely because

(A) a teacher in Wales does not often consider
transferring to Africa
(B) he was well aware of the financial liabilities
of moving to a new continent
(C) the caller's needs were transparent from the
beginning of the conversation
(D) he would never accept a job from a person
who had confused two countries
(E) everyone knew that he was in financial
trouble and needed a new job

45. The phrase "I have a job in Arfreekah" in lines
42-43 conveys the author's sense of

(A) unrealistic speculation
(B) playful optimism
(C) objective reasoning
(D) profound musing
(E) euphoric celebration

46. In the context of the passage, the author "was in
a panic" (line 51) most likely because he

(A) thought that the scenery in Africa was less
picturesque than that of his home country
(B) hadn't spent enough time learning about the
African continent and its customs
(C) feared the rough descent that was sure to
come from the small plane
(D) had failed to consider the magnitude of the
change he was making
(E) knew that the plane was entering an area of
dangerously strong winds

47. In lines 59-74 ("It was . . . forever") which of the
following rhetorical devices does the author use?

(A) Ironic understatement
(B) Illustrative anachronism
(C) Sensory description
(D) Didactic allegory
(E) Sensual hyperbole

48. Lines 74-78 ("I had . . . return") express a sense
of

(A) whimsical excitement
(B) sincere belonging
(C) lethargic tranquility
(D) immediate submission
(E) environmental concern

Answer Key: PART 5

Part 5

PASSAGE 1

1. D
2. D
3. A
4. D
5. D
6. C
7. B
8. A

PASSAGE 2

9. A
10. A
11. C
12 B
13. E
14. E
15. D
16. A
17. B

PASSAGE 3

18. E
19. E
20. D
21. C
22. B
23. C
24. A
25. A
26. E
27. A
28. D
29. D

PASSAGE 4

30. E
31. C
32. B
33. D
34. C
35. A
36. E
37. A
38. D
39 E

PASSAGE 5

40. C
41. A
42. C
43. B
44. A
45. B
46. D
47. C
48. B

Need an answer explained? Send the page number and the
question number to **info@ilexpublications.com**, and we
will send you a full analysis and explanation.

Post-Test Analysis

This post-test analysis is essential if you want to see an improvement on your next test. Possible reasons for errors on the five passages in this section are listed here. Place check marks next to the types of errors that pertain to you, or write your own types of errors in the blank spaces.

LONG READING PASSAGE 1:   # Correct: _____   # Wrong: _____   # Unanswered: _____

◇   Did not understand the questions or answers
◇   Did not understand the line references
◇   Read too much or too little around the line references
◇   Did not create effective margin answers
◇   Did not use process of elimination
◇   Could not find evidence to answer the questions
◇   Could not choose between two possible answers
◇   Could not comprehend the topic of the passage
◇   Interpreted the passage rather than using evidence
Other: _____

LONG READING PASSAGE 2:   # Correct: _____   # Wrong: _____   # Unanswered: _____

◇   Did not understand the questions or answers
◇   Did not understand the line references
◇   Read too much or too little around the line references
◇   Did not create effective margin answers
◇   Did not use process of elimination
◇   Could not find evidence to answer the questions
◇   Could not choose between two possible answers
◇   Could not comprehend the topic of the passage
◇   Interpreted the passage rather than using evidence
◇   Other: _____

> **Use this form** to better analyze your performance. If you don't understand why you made errors, there is no way that you can correct them!

LONG READING PASSAGE 3:   # Correct: _____   # Wrong: _____   # Unanswered: _____

◇   Did not understand the questions or answers
◇   Did not understand the line references
◇   Read too much or too little around the line references
◇   Did not create effective margin answers
◇   Did not use process of elimination
◇   Could not find evidence to answer the questions
◇   Could not choose between two possible answers
◇   Could not comprehend the topic of the passage
◇   Interpreted the passage rather than using evidence
Other: _____

Continue to the next page.

Post-Test Analysis

This post-test analysis is essential if you want to see an improvement on your next test. Possible reasons for errors on the five passages in this section are listed here. Place check marks next to the types of errors that pertain to you, or write your own types of errors in the blank spaces.

LONG READING PASSAGE 4:   **# Correct:** _____   **# Wrong:** _____   **# Unanswered:** _____

◇   Did not understand the questions or answers
◇   Did not understand the line references
◇   Read too much or too little around the line references
◇   Did not create effective margin answers
◇   Did not use process of elimination
◇   Could not find evidence to answer the questions
◇   Could not choose between two possible answers
◇   Could not comprehend the topic of the passage
◇   Interpreted the passage rather than using evidence
Other: _____

> **Use this form** to better analyze your performance. If you don't understand why you made errors, there is no way that you can correct them!

LONG READING PASSAGE 5:   **# Correct:** _____   **# Wrong:** _____   **# Unanswered:** _____

◇   Did not understand the questions or answers
◇   Did not understand the line references
◇   Read too much or too little around the line references
◇   Did not create effective margin answers
◇   Did not use process of elimination
◇   Could not find evidence to answer the questions
◇   Could not choose between two possible answers
◇   Could not comprehend the topic of the passage
◇   Interpreted the passage rather than using evidence
◇   Other: _____

TRY ALL OF OUR ADVANCED PRACTICE SERIES BOOKS

If you like this easy-to-use workbook, check out our other great volumes. The *Reading Comprehension Workbook, Part II* is part of the *IES Advanced Practice Series*, which currently includes a *Critical Reading Workbook*, a *Math Workbook*, a *Grammar Workbook*, and the soon to be released *New 2016 SAT Workbook*. Please visit www.ILEXpublications.com to order these resources, or find our complete line of SAT workbooks on Amazon.com.

Made in the USA
Lexington, KY
15 November 2016